Workplace Innovation in Canada

JACQUIE MANSELL

Workplace Innovation in Canada

Reflections on the Past...
Prospects for the Future

Ministry of Education, Ontario
Information Centre, 13th Floor,
Mowat Block, Queen's Park,
Toronto, Ont.   M7A 1L2

The findings of this study are the personal responsibility of the author and, as such, have not been endorsed by the Members of the Economic Council of Canada.

©Minister of Supply and Services Canada 1987

Available in Canada through

Associated Bookstores
and other booksellers

or by mail from

Canadian Government Publishing Centre
Supply and Services Canada
Ottawa, Canada K1A 0S9

| Catalogue No. EC22-146/1987E | Canada: $4.95 |
| ISBN 0-660-12554-4 | Other Countries: $5.95 |

Price subject to change without notice

All rights reserved. No part of this publication may be reproduced, stored in a retrieval system, or transmitted by any means, electronic, mechanical, photocopying, recording or otherwise, without the prior written permission of the Publishing Services, Canadian Government Publishing Centre, Ottawa, Canada K1A 0S9.

Cette étude est également disponible en français sous le titre : *L'innovation en milieu de travail au Canada.*

Contents

	Acknowledgments	vii
	Foreword	ix
1	Introduction	1
2	**Fifteen Years of Innovation: 1970-85**	3
	Pre-1975: A Focus on Satisfaction and Communications	3
	Job Design – The Happy Worker	3
	Joint Committees – The Informed Worker	4
	Post-1975: A Focus on Participation and Total System Effectiveness	5
	Parallel Structures – The Involved Worker	7
	Socio-Technical Systems – The Effective Organization	12
3	**Fifteen Years Ahead: Prospects for the Future**	21
	Learnings from the Past	21
	Tensions between Workplace Innovation and Larger Society	22
	Management Prerogatives and Corporate Policy	22
	Collective Bargaining and Job Control	22
	Conditions for Linking the Micro and Macro Levels	23
	Experience at the Micro Level	23
	The Legal Framework of Collective Bargaining	26
	Broader Societal Changes	27
	Current Developments at the Macro Level	28
4	Concluding Remarks	31
	Notes	33
	Glossary	35
	Bibliography	37

Acknowledgments

The author wishes to give special thanks to Tom Rankin for the innumerable, long, intense, illuminating, and stimulating discussions and debates that went into every phase of the creation of this study. Thanks are also due to Gordon Betcherman, Kathryn McMullen, and Keith Newton for many helpful comments and suggestions. Ultimately, of course, the biases, errors, and omissions belong to the author alone.

Foreword

Technological change is vitally important to Canada. It is through technological change that productivity growth occurs and productivity growth leads to gains in output, income, and employment. Technological change also brings fundamental adjustments in industry structure and in work.

Research to date on the impacts of technological change on the labour market, while voluminous, suffers from a number of shortcomings. Much of it is partial, in the sense of treating a particular technology, industry, or region; some of it is partisan, in the sense of following a single ideological line; much of it is speculative, lacking in empirical content; and much of it is foreign. In light of these shortcomings, the Economic Council of Canada, through its Labour Market Impacts of Technological Change program of research, has addressed a wide range of issues relating to labour markets and technological change. The range of topics includes the overall employment effects of technological change, historically and into the future; the occupational and income effects; innovation in Canada; and the relationship between technological and organizational change.

The research findings are discussed in two companion reports. The first consists of a Statement by the Council, entitled *Making Technology Work* (1987). It highlights the major policy issues and sets out, in its last section, a strategic policy framework. The second – *Innovation and Jobs in Canada* (1987) – discusses the research in fuller detail. In addition, there are a number of related background studies of which this is one.

There is a tendency for people to equate technological change with new/improved products and production processes, that is, with "hard" technology. But there is another, equally important element that consists of changes in management techniques and in organizational design, of changes in how work is organized and in how workers and management relate. It is with this question of "soft" technological change that this study is concerned.

Organizational change can take many forms. In this study, one approach in particular – socio-technical systems – is examined in some detail. The socio-technical systems (STS) approach explicitly incorporates the needs of both technical and social (human) aspects of organizational design. Our interest in STS stems from an observation that effective technological change within a firm can only occur when the technical and human components of production are combined in such a way that the one complements the other. Failure to get both right will mean that the maximum benefits made possible by technological change will not be realized.

The author, Jacquie Mansell, is an independent researcher and consultant based in Toronto. She was formerly senior consultant with the Ontario Quality of Working Life Centre.

Judith Maxwell
Chairman

1 Introduction

"Innovation in work organization is turning out to be as important as technology" – so concluded the "Interim Report to the Human Resource Task Force on the Automotive Industry" (The Canada Consulting Group, 1985). For an industry that knows it must change or die, such a finding is fundamental.

Meanwhile, in Halifax, Pratt and Whitney is constructing a new plant that will use, not only the latest technology, but also the most innovative of work organizations. The organization will be designed so that the workers will be "multifunctional and versatile." They will get involved in all aspects of the work, including the management of the complex tools and systems that control production. The reason for this innovative work organization, according to Gilles Ouimet, Pratt and Whitney's senior vice-president of operations, is simple: "If we do not do this, it is ball game over, five or ten years down the road" (*The Globe and Mail*, July 3, 1985).

And in Bromont, Quebec, in their first year of operating one of the most technologically advanced plants in the country, Canadian General Electric employees each pocketed over $1,000 in productivity bonuses. Decisions in the plant are made by consensus via a set of interlocking, self-managing teams. Workers are encouraged to develop their skills to the highest degree possible, and responsibility and authority are pushed down to the lowest level possible. In the first year of the plant's operation, this "radical" organization design resulted in an overall performance 20 per cent above expectations and losses (scrap and rework) 50 per cent below expectations (McGill Human Resource Associates, 1985).

At a time when Canada is faced with some tough economic, social, and political problems, the above "snapshots" would seem to offer exciting possibilities. Yet, against the uproar of discussion on new technology, the interest in workplace innovation is barely more than a whisper. However, 15 years of experience with such innovation in Canada has repeatedly indicated that what is at stake in new organization designs is critical to management, labour, and government.

This study discusses the experiences in this country, since the late 1960s, with workplace innovation. Illustrations are given of many of the more common approaches to change – from the more limited forms focusing primarily on communications and the nature of individual jobs to more "radical" approaches involving widespread participation in management and even total organization redesign.

The development of the workplace innovation field over the past 15 to 20 years is examined in relation to changes in the broader economic, social, and political environment. A number of key lessons are summarized from the experience of the last two decades. Finally, the study explores some of the conditions, at both the micro level of the organization and, more broadly, the macro level of society, that may be necessary, with reference in particular to the unionized sector, for the potential of new work forms to develop further in Canada.

2 Fifteen Years of Innovation: 1970-85

In May 1980 a group of about 30 trade unionists, managers, academics, and government people from across Canada met in Toronto to discuss the possibility of hosting an international conference on the quality of working life. The idea was a bold one – was there really enough interest, expertise, and commitment within Canada to support such an ambitious undertaking? However, the group decided enthusiastically to go ahead and in August-September 1981 approximately 1,700 people, including roughly 1,000 managers and more than 250 union representatives from over 20 countries, gathered in Toronto to discuss world developments in workplace innovation. By far the largest group of participants at the conference, including many of the organizers and presenters, were Canadians. There was no longer any doubt that as a nation Canada was seriously engaged in a search for new approaches to the challenges of the workplace.

Over the past 15 years, both interest and activity in the area of workplace innovation have been steadily growing in Canada. Since the late 1960s, leaders from management, labour, and government, each in their own way, have expressed concern with the bottom-line performance of Canadian enterprises, the quality of people's work experiences, and labour-management relations across the country (Hunnius, ed., 1971; *The Labour Gazette*, 1978). However, the way these concerns have been defined and, hence, the approaches taken to their resolution have been continually shaped by larger developments in the economic, social, and political environment.

Pre-1975: A Focus on Satisfaction and Communications

In the late 1960s and early 1970s most of the workplace innovation was initiated by management, motivated by the dual objectives of "productivity improvement" and "humanization of work." Influenced by such management theorists as Herzberg et al. (1959) and Likert (1967), progressive managers believed that there was a causal connection between the above goals in the direction of "a happier worker is a more productive worker." Innovation was seen as necessary in order to change crucial attitudes and relations in the workplace. Bottom-line improvements were sought in the areas of absenteeism, turnover, recruitment, and labour relations (e.g., fewer grievances and work stoppages). Innovation generally focused on increasing employee job satisfaction and morale as the means by which to achieve both these bottom-line objectives and a more humane workplace. The most common workplace innovations during this period were some form of job redesign and/or communication program (Mansell et al., 1978; White, 1979).

Job Design – The Happy Worker

Job redesign, which involves the rotation, enlargement, or enrichment of individual jobs, was more common in (although not exclusive to) non-union organizations where it was usually designed and implemented by management alone in a "top-down" manner. Most early job design programs were implemented in only a part of the operation, usually in an area where job satisfaction and morale were considered to be unusually low. In job rotation and enlargement schemes, the number of separate tasks a worker performs is increased, but the level of skill and authority or autonomy required to perform the tasks does not change. Job enrichment, however, while normally still focusing on the individual job, does involve the addition of more skilled and responsible tasks (such as basic planning, scheduling, and administrative tasks) to the job.

Job rotation and enlargement schemes, by themselves, were (and still are) most common in unskilled and semi-skilled assembly, clerical, and warehousing work. Job rotation is often managed in a very informal manner, being guided by the preferences of the workers involved and immediate production conditions such as the amount of rework, overtime, etc. For example, in Domtar's corrugated container plant in Toronto, all production workers rotate between machines two to three times daily. The workers control their own rotations and the better workers and foremen do the training. Although not all the workers like to rotate, generally job rotation is considered a success as it has resulted in a more skilled, flexible, and less fatigued work force. The program began in 1973 and in 1977 the plant manager reported that the plant had higher productivity than other similar plants in Ontario (Mansell et al., 1978).

Job enlargement, which usually includes some job rotation, became particularly popular in the 1970s in the electronics industry where it is well-suited to the technical system of modular assembly. At National Cash Register in Waterloo, Ontario, there are four assembly lines each producing one of four basic modules that make up the product. The technology has been adapted in such a way that each line is made up of individual work stations where an assembler installs several components to make an identifiable assembly. At each station, four to five different tools are used to perform several different operations. Assemblers choose their own tools, decide when to change a tool, set their own work pace, and may request alterations to work station layout. Everyone on a line is trained to work at every station on the line and people rotate regularly. Assemblers also work under a variable hours system that allows them to vary their daily starting and finishing time, within limits. Plant management reports that the job enlargement scheme has resulted in better product quality control and greater employee job satisfaction (Mansell et al., 1978).

Similar job enlargement programs have also become common in data-processing operations. For example, in 1980 the Union of Postal Communications Employees and Canada Post undertook a joint quality-of-working-life (QWL) project in the Data Conversion Division of the Computer Operations Branch of the Canada Post headquarters in Ottawa. This division converted information from financial and other documents to punched cards and diskettes using TAB 405, IBM 129, 3741, and 3742 machines. As a major part of the project, the employees and supervisors redesigned their jobs to include more training and job rotation and less direct supervision of employees. They also changed working hours to allow more flexible starting and finishing times. These changes led to a more equitable distribution of overtime, a significant improvement in absenteeism, and measured improvements in perceived autonomy and job satisfaction (Andrew, 1982).

Job enrichment, on the other hand, developed more quickly in financial institutions, insurance companies, and service industries where the work is such that there are a series of related tasks involved in the servicing of a specific client or client group (Rosenbaum and Dresner, 1979; Mansell et al., 1978; White, 1979). At Prudential Insurance, for example, between 1973 and 1977, jobs were redesigned in 12 sections of the company's operation in Toronto. In these sections, both the technical and social systems were modified to enable all employees to be trained to do a whole job, from filing their own papers to direct contact with clients. The whole jobs were broken down into a series of steps and as employees progressed, at their own pace, to the top level functions, their pay increased. People were also trained to be able to fill in for each other when necessary. The results of job enrichment were increased opportunities for advancement for employees, reduced staffing due to increased productivity, improved employee job satisfaction and morale, decreased turnover and training costs, reduced absenteeism, and more management time freed for planning (Mansell et al., 1978).

In a very different setting, the city of Calgary also redesigned some jobs in its Sanitation Department. For example, residential garbage pickup was redesigned so that one person was responsible for driving, loading, and all other aspects of servicing a specific collection route. This redesign improved both morale and productivity (White, 1979).

Job enrichment has also been applied successfully in manufacturing settings, such as the two pet food plants of General Foods in Cobourg, Ontario. Both plants are continuous process operations and the newer plant is very capital intensive. In the older dry pet food plant, jobs were redesigned and in the new intermediate moist plant they were designed from the start to include a variety of related tasks involving preparatory, quality control, and housekeeping functions. The job enrichment concept was taken the farthest in the warehousing area of the new plant where there is only one job classification and all the workers do all the jobs in the area. The workers also do much of the paperwork that would traditionally be a foreman's responsibility, and the position of warehouse group leader has been eliminated. The foreman plays more of a planning role; workers are told generally what is expected of them and they handle the day-to-day routine themselves, in their own way. These innovations have resulted in a reduction in the number of workers needed in the older facility (achieved through attrition), greatly increased sanitation in the older facility, and increased productivity. Most people like the variety, feel more pride in their work, and, where there is job rotation, they like being able to help each other (Mansell et al., 1978).

Joint Committees – The Informed Worker

Another common focus of innovation in the 1960s and early 1970s was communications. Many shop-floor and establishment-wide problems, ranging from absenteeism and high scrap rates to active sabotage and strikes, were defined as morale problems and blamed on poor communications. Early communications programs (some dating back as far as the war years) were designed primarily to improve employee/union-management relations and to boost morale by giving employees more feedback on the performance of their work area and of the company overall, and by providing the union and/or workers with a more informal, less adversarial forum to air their concerns. Although the terms participation, consultation, and involvement were often used, few of the early programs involved any significant changes in decision-making powers (Mansell et al., 1978; White, 1979).

The usual forum for information exchange was regular meetings between workers and managers at the level of both the establishment as a whole and the particular work area. In the 1960s and early 1970s, it was fairly common in unionized settings to establish a union-management committee, composed of the local union executive and local senior management, that would meet on a regular basis between contract negotiations (see Labour Canada, various years). The purpose of these committees was to improve relations between union and management through a general sharing of information, and sometimes to provide a forum for on-going problem resolution (but not grievance resolution) during the term of the contract. For example, Molson's Brewery in Lethbridge, Alberta, has a committee of seven management and seven union representatives who meet monthly to deal with current items of interest ranging from marketing problems to proposed technological changes (White, 1979). In the 1970s, there were also many large, complex organizations that established both establishment-wide and area level committees to help deal with some of the problems of size and diversity (for example, Ontario Hydro, St. Thomas Psychiatric Hospital, Red Deer College, University of Alberta, Edmonton General Hospital, Alberta Department of Agriculture, etc.).

Finally, some large organizations have also established union-management committees at the enterprise level, often as a way to deal with particularly difficult labour relations situations. Both Ontario Hydro and the International Nickel Company of Canada established such committees in the early 1970s after prolonged periods of poor labour-management relations. In the 1980s, labour-management committees for information exchange are becoming more common in the public sector. Most ministries of the Ontario government, for example, have what are called employee relations committees, often at both the ministry level and the local level. A good example of such a committee is the Alberta Department of Education which has a formally established 13-member committee consisting of the deputy minister, director, and assistant director of personnel, and 10 employee representatives from the various branches of the department. The committee meets regularly to discuss a wide range of topics and recommend policies to management, and to provide information for employees (White, 1979).

Reports on joint committees at all levels are usually positive, although generally quite subjective. Both union and management report improvements in communications and labour-management relations, which they believe are reflected in smoother negotiations, better grievance resolution, and fewer strikes. They say the committees enable them to better understand each other, to deal more directly with problems before they fester and grow, and to pool their information and expertise in tackling difficult issues (Mansell et al., 1978; Mansell, 1980*b*; White, 1979; *Quality of Working Life: The Canadian Scene*, 1984). Based on such extensive, positive experience with labour-management committees in both Canada and the United States, by the late 1970s the federal government and the provincial governments of Alberta, New Brunswick, and Ontario had established formal programs to help support the establishment of various levels of joint committees in their jurisdictions. For example, the Preventative Mediation Program of the province of Ontario has helped to establish an average of eight to ten "joint action committees" annually since 1979 (Ontario Ministry of Labour, 1984).

Establishment-wide joint committees are also common in non-union settings (for example, Syncrude Canada, Esso Resources, Canadian Tire Corporation, Lincoln Electric, Supreme Aluminum Industries, etc.). However, there is considerable debate in the field as to whether such committee structures actually are "innovative" forms of workplace democracy (Nightingale, 1982) or no more than traditional substitutes for an independent, legally constituted union. Indeed, there is evidence, documented most clearly in the case of Supreme Aluminum Industries, one of the best-known non-union Canadian firms with such a joint committee, that the power of worker representatives is significantly limited in situations where there is no legally rooted, separate power base for the workers and no independent mechanisms to ensure rights of due process (Mansell, 1977 and 1980*b*; Nightingale, 1984; Bernstein, 1976).

Post-1975: A Focus on Participation and Total System Effectiveness

Although job design and communications-oriented programs still exist in many organizations, by the mid- to late 1970s, the major focus of workplace innovation in Canada had begun to shift. Problems in the workplace were becoming much more acute. Both Canadian manufacturing and primary resource industries were beginning to be hit hard by international economic conditions, not the least of which was tough foreign competition. In reaction to the need to be more competitive, managers were starting to seriously re-examine their organizations as a whole. The earlier objective of "productivity improvement" was now being redefined more broadly as a need for greater "organizational effectiveness."

Changes were developing in world market structures and in technological capabilities that were both pushing and enabling organizations to focus much more on quality, flexibility, and integration (Reich, 1983; Hirschhorn, 1984; Piore, 1985; Wheelwright, 1985). In addition, by the early 1980s it had become clear that technological upgrading would have to play a major role in any attempt on the part of Canadian industry to remain competitive (see, for example, Employment and Immigration Canada, 1986). Hence, for the first time, by the 1980s the nature of technology and technological change became a significant issue with respect to workplace innovation.

It was becoming obvious, from both theory and practice, that approaches focusing on the single job and limited primarily to the shop or office floor could not deal with the more serious challenges of the 1980s. Managers also realized they would need more than "satisfied" employees in order to achieve the more fundamental technological and organizational changes now required. They knew that change would be extremely difficult, if not impossible, unless all employees, management and nonmanagement, were willing and able to be open and flexible. By the mid-1970s, one of the key things that had been learned from both European and North American experience with organization change was that active participation is one of the most effective ways of overcoming resistance to change (Katzell and Yankelovich, 1975; Emery and Thorsrud, 1976; Strauss, 1977). In addition, many managers also realized (admittedly, aided by a popular fascination with Japanese management techniques) that the chances of finding workable solutions to many organization problems would be greater if the experience and expertise resident at all levels of the organization could be drawn upon.

Hence, between 1970 and 1980, management's orientation shifted away from job satisfaction towards more employee involvement and participation, as a means of both increasing openness to change and improving upon the potential quality of change (for example, see Brown, 1978; Hemsworth, 1979; and Bennett, 1980). At the same time, many managers began to look beyond pilot projects, or experiments in parts of the organization, towards what might be done to improve the organization as a total system (for numerous illustrations, see Cunningham and White, eds., 1984).

The change in management orientation was reinforced by pressures from the trade union movement. By the early 1970s, trade unions in North America had begun to formulate their own views on workplace innovation – partly in response to the fairly high profile and often dramatic statements that management, government, and academics were making about the problems of "blue-collar blues" (see, for example, U.S. Department of Health, Education and Welfare Task Force, 1973), and partly because of problems that they themselves were experiencing in relation to their members (for example, apathy towards the union, difficulties in getting contracts ratified, and increases in wildcat strikes). In addition, many trade union leaders were sincerely concerned with the boredom and oversupervision that characterized the work of many of their members (Bluestone, 1977a; Reimer, 1979).

Generally, trade unionists were suspicious of the job enrichment and communications orientations to workplace innovation. Much of the language and practice of the job satisfaction/work humanization approach was seen by them as too elitist, paternalistic, productivity-oriented and, above all, anti-union (Barbash, 1977; Winpisinger, 1973; Docquier, 1977a). They were much more interested in an approach that would build upon the trade union tradition of democratization of the workplace. They had also learned from many years of experience with various forms of joint committees that, despite their benefits, there were limits to what could be achieved via committees that did not have a sharing of decision-making powers as an explicit, agreed upon goal. Therefore, in the 1970s some trade unionists began to specify what conditions they required in order to support and/or participate in workplace innovations. They began to call for an approach that reinforced the role of the trade union in the workplace, was based on the active participation of workers in all phases of any change, and involved a real redistribution of decision-making powers in areas of substantive interest to workers (Ephlin, 1973; Bluestone, 1977b; Reimer, 1979; United Auto Workers, 1979; United Steelworkers of America, 1978).

Perhaps what is most notable about the development of workplace innovation in Canada in the 1970s is the amount of attention given to it by government. In the mid-1970s, both the federal government and the government of Ontario expended a tremendous amount of time, money, and political energy to establish formal programs to promote and support the quality-of-working-life concept. There were three major broad policy reasons for the high level of government interest and activity: 1) concern with reducing the high level of industrial conflict that had won Canada the unwelcome distinction of having one of the worst industrial relations records among Western industrialized countries; 2) concern with increasing the productivity and, hence, competitive position of Canadian enterprises; and 3) concern with improving the overall quality of life by reducing alienation and promoting personal fulfilment and increased job satisfaction (Adams, 1981).

Although it would be misleading to imply that management, labour, and government had the same orientation to workplace innovation, by the late 1970s they had at least found enough "common ground" to give the field not only a new direction, but also a significant shot of new energy. Probably the clearest expression of this energy and direction is in the unanimous recommendation made in January 1978 to the Ontario Minister of Labour by an advisory committee of senior trade union and management leaders in the province:

> ... We wish to say that all members have found it useful and rewarding to learn about the meaning and application of QWL concepts.... We have concluded that QWL is much more than an abstract academic notion or gimmick. We have found that effective QWL projects are firmly rooted in the real world of industrial relations....
>
> ... We found that many experiments occurring in Ontario and elsewhere do not qualify as true QWL projects. For instance, the establishment of joint labour-management committees to improve communications, the elimination of incentive pay and the substitution of group bonus plans, provisions for employee participation in productivity gains (Scanlon-type plans) – none of these, whatever their merits, are true QWL projects.
>
> From our investigations, we have concluded that a true quality of working life project must:
>
> a) provide for genuine worker participation in the planning or restructuring of the work process, with a view to accommodating and reconciling human needs on the one hand and the technical requirements of the particular enterprise, on the other, so that the worker is able to achieve more variety, scope, and autonomy in the performance of his duties; and
>
> b) a concomitant change in management attitudes and practices, away from an authoritarian mode towards a more facilitative, consultative, and advisory role.
>
> ... Where the above conditions are met, we are convinced there is scope for real advancement, with benefits accruing to the entire enterprise. That is why we believe it is in the interests of management and labour alike that a substantial program be set up to promote and encourage quality of working life experiments on a wide front (Ontario Quality of Working Life Advisory Committee, 1978).

Two new forms of workplace innovation, both of which are consistent (although in different ways) with the orientations outlined above, and both of which can be seen as extensions on earlier orientations towards communications and job design, have been steadily increasing in Canada since the late 1970s. The first new form focuses on the creation of an additional set of parallel structures within the existing organization as a vehicle for greater union and/or employee participation. It encompasses a number of similar approaches, including quality control (QC) circles, employee involvement (EI) programs, many of the joint committees that go under the QWL label, and problem-solving groups that commonly develop out of programs specifically designed to improve union-management relations (e.g., intergroup, relationships by objectives, and preventative mediation). The second new form of innovation is the socio-technical systems (STS) approach to job and organization design and redesign. That approach focuses on making fundamental changes to existing traditional values, structures, and processes of organizations. At the level of the primary work system, it is most commonly characterized by the establishment of semi-autonomous, or self-regulating, work groups.

Parallel Structures – The Involved Worker

The establishment of parallel participative structures is a natural marriage of two techniques long popular in North America – the suggestion scheme and the communications meeting. Given the concerns being expressed by management, labour, and government in the mid-1970s, this approach is a logical extension of the communications-oriented joint committee approach common in the 1960s and early 1970s. Management clearly wanted more than purely "motivational" approaches to productivity. They were anxious to deal directly with productivity and product quality issues on the shop-floor and were, therefore, fascinated by the Japanese experience with quality circles (for abundant evidence, see any management or business publication in the late 1970s). Management also saw participation as a way to get more worker support for necessary changes in both technology and work methods (Canadian Manufacturers' Association, 1982; Vivian, 1983).

At the same time, parallel participative structures seemed to provide an opportunity for unions and workers to become involved in issues of real importance to them, without interfering with traditional collective bargaining. Although still opposed to any program focusing narrowly on productivity, by the late 1970s many unions were also being hurt by the non-competitive position of Canadian enterprise and were much more open to exploring productivity and quality concerns and technological change with management (see United Steelworkers of America, 1982). As a condition for supporting these programs, unions usually insisted that they be designed and administered jointly by union and management, that the local union leadership play an active role in the program, that the programs be kept separate from the collective bargaining process, and that joint committees be given real powers to deal with issues of concern to the workers (see Bluestone, 1977b; Watts, 1982; Reimer, 1979). In fact, by the early 1980s it was not uncommon for unions themselves to initiate such programs (for example, OPSEU Local 307; USWA Local 6855, UAW Local 707, and ECWU Local 39). For their part, governments were so hungry for improvements in labour relations that they were happy to support almost any program that union and management would agree to participate in jointly. They were especially supportive if the programs were aimed at improving the effectiveness of Canadian organizations.

For the above reasons, the parallel participative structures approach is undoubtedly the most common approach to workplace innovation in Canada in the 1980s. It is especially popular in the auto industry (e.g., Ford, General Motors, Budd, Wean United, Clark Equipment, TRW, Bendix) where in major corporations such as Ford and General Motors it is even incorporated into master collective agreements and mandated by American head offices as part of corporate policy. The approach is also common in other manufacturing and resource industries, as well as in a diversity of government and service organizations (e.g., General Foods, Polysar, American Cyanamid, Forano, B.C. Forest Products, Jordan and Ste. Michelle Cellars Ltd., Norton Company, Ontario Paper Company, Air Canada, Luscar Sterco Mining, Union Gas, Westinghouse, Bell Telephone, Town of Dundas, City of Calgary, Harbour Castle Hilton, and a range of health care settings). In fact, a recent American study estimated that over 90 per cent of the *Fortune 500* companies now have some form of QC program (Lawler and Mohrman, 1985). However, in most organizations, parallel participative structures are implemented slowly, area-by-area, so that it is very common for only a part of the organization to be affected by the innovation (for example, see Austrom and Graffi, 1984).

Most programs based on a parallel participative structures approach consist of a two-tiered system of joint union/employee-management committees. There is normally an establishment level "steering committee" and one or more area level committees. The steering committee is usually composed of several senior managers and either the local union executive or, in non-union settings, elected or management selected employee representatives. Normally, the role of the steering committee is to oversee the operation of the area level committees and to deal with establishment-wide issues. The area level committees are almost always completely voluntary – no area need have a committee and no individual (with the exception of area management) need participate. They are usually composed of 8 to 12 workers, often led by a supervisor or facilitator, and generally meet at very regular intervals – generally one hour per week or one day per every four to six weeks. The term "participative management" is sometimes used to label this approach.

Most area level committees deal primarily with issues related to immediate working conditions, productivity and product quality, and (where permitted) health and safety. Although "pure" QC circles are meant to focus exclusively on productivity and quality problems, in practice many QC programs (particularly in unionized settings) allow for the discussion of a much broader range of topics. In fact, in practice there is often little difference between the operation of QC circles, EI programs, and the joint problem-solving groups often established following establishment-wide intergroup or relationships-by-objectives programs. The only significant difference is that the problem-solving groups have grown out of an explicit, formal attempt to improve labour-management relations. Regardless of the type of program, in unionized settings area committees are usually not permitted to discuss issues related to the collective agreement. Finally, most area level committees are given some form of special training in problem resolution, often at a fairly sophisticated level (e.g., in statistical process control, SPC).

Perhaps the best-known "participative management" programs in Canada are the quality-of-working-life and employee involvement programs of General Motors and Ford (Bennett, 1980; Jenkins, 1981). Although General Motors has a large number of QWL sites in its U.S. operations, GM UAW locals in Canada have generally refused to participate, primarily because they do not trust the attitudes and motives of management. As a result, there has been very little QWL activity within GM Canada.

In contrast, Ford Canada does have some very impressive QWL success stories to tell. For example, four of the five plants of Ford Canada's operation in Windsor, Ontario, have active QWL or EI programs. Management and UAW Local 200 at the Ford Windsor Casting Plant first started their QWL program in early 1982 because they were concerned with the survival of the plant. The plant is an iron foundry manufacturing engine blocks and employs about 1,200 people. The structure of the project consists of a joint union-management plant level steering committee; several subcommittees of the steering committee, involving managers, supervisors, shop-floor union representatives, skilled tradesmen, and operators; and a growing number of area committees made up of volunteering supervisors, operators, and tradesmen.

Area committees, usually made up of about 12 people, focus on work-related issues and devise plans that are implemented during regular work hours.

Some of the achievements of these committees have been the creation of a quality control bulletin board; improved cafeteria services; the construction of an ambulance station; better access methods to stewards; improved methods for setting preventative maintenance priorities; improved procedures for issuing protective clothing; several technical system changes designed to make the production process both safer and more efficient, including the development of a cheaper waste-metal recycling technique; better housekeeping; and some joint union-management social events. The "bottom line" on these achievements is impressive. Production cost savings attributable to the QWL program are estimated at more than a million dollars per year. Health and safety activities and working conditions have improved, as have union-management and supervisor-operator relations. Three years after its start up, both union and management were happy with and committed to their program (*Windsor Star*, 1983; *The Toronto Star*, 1984; joint presentation by union and management of the Ford Windsor Casting Plant in London, Ontario, April 1984).

The American Cyanamid Company and the Energy and Chemical Workers Local 21 have also had considerable success with parallel participative structures. The Cyanamid plant, located in Welland, Ontario, employs approximately 750 people in a continuous process operation that produces fertilizers and other chemicals. In 1980, the company and union agreed to jointly develop a quality-of-working-life program in an attempt to deal with serious problems of high absenteeism, poor quality, and bad relations within the plant. Two departments were chosen as the pilot sites for the program. Both sites were chosen because they were key areas with advancing technology and young, dissatisfied workers ready for change. Union, management, and the workers in the pilot sites decided jointly on what form their program would take. They chose a four-level system of committees for information sharing and participative decision making: a steering committee composed of local and corporate management representatives and local and national union representatives; a plant-wide committee with representatives from all levels in the plant (management, union, foremen, and workers); business teams with members from all levels and functions connected to a department; and shift teams made up of a foreman and hourly workers from a shift.

The business teams and shift teams began operating in the two pilot departments in early 1983. By the end of 1983, the company estimated that the QWL programs in the two departments had resulted in total savings of $372,000, due to lower turnover, fewer grievances, a significant reduction in downtime, a 7 per cent productivity improvement, and over 130 ideas from workers for modifying the technical system to improve the efficiency of the production process. The people in the departments also report marked improvements in their problem-solving skills and in communications and relationships between operations and maintenance, between operators and foremen, and between shifts. In addition, the union president believes the program has been instrumental in awakening interest in the union among younger workers. It is also significant that although the QWL program is experiencing problems due to a serious downturn in the economic position of the plant, it is surviving (Arnopoulos, 1983; List, 1985).

In a totally different setting, the city of Calgary has also implemented a highly successful productivity program using a system of joint union-management committees. In the fall of 1982, experimental productivity programs were initiated by union and management within three divisions of the city's Engineering Department, including the division responsible for the construction and maintenance of the transmission and distribution water lines within the city. Surveys were used to identify areas of common concern in each of the divisions and committees of volunteer managers, union members, and staff specialists were given the mandate to address specific problem areas and recommend solutions to senior management via a site-wide joint committee. Within one year, the results of the program were dramatic. In 1983 and 1984, the Engineering Department realized nearly $4 million in productivity improvements, most of which was generated primarily by the three experimental programs. One of the three program areas saved approximately $1.4 million in improved productivity and lower unit costs due to its program in the first year of its operation. Most of the savings came through changes to equipment, work procedures, and scheduling. The same area also improved its safety statistics to the point of winning its departmental safety award. On the strength of this success, the Engineering Department has expanded its program and the city as a whole has launched an ambitious service improvement program (Sheehy, 1985).

Consistent with the above case illustrations, the overwhelming experience with quality control circles and employee involvement programs is that when given the opportunity to participate, employees are greatly concerned with productivity and product quality. Most forms of participative problem solving have generated numerous suggestions, most often focusing on modifications to the technology or technical system, for improving the efficiency and quality of the production process. The results have usually been significant bottom-line savings. In this respect, even when technological change was not an explicit focus of a change program, management's hopes that participation might help to support such change have been abundantly realized.

Many managers and unionists are quickly recognizing this important connection, which reflects the fact that both management and labour have a major stake in what happens in relation to technological change in the workplace. They both also greatly affect the success or failure of any change. Joint participation in everything from the choosing of new technology through to its ongoing monitoring and evaluation helps to get the commitment of both parties, to ensure that the needs of both management and the workers are taken into account, and to get the greatest number of good ideas brought to bear on the change process.

In fact, most trade unions are now calling for union participation, usually via the use of parallel participative structures (although they would not use this term), in all stages of any technological change (Surich, 1985; United Steelworkers of America, n.d.), and many organizations have begun to use this approach. For example, in British Columbia, where the forestry industry is undergoing large-scale modernization, the International Woodworkers of America have worked jointly with the management of several companies to ensure that new technology was adopted in the most effective manner – for the business and for the people (for example, Lakeland Mills sawmill in Prince George and B.C. Forest Products' Hammond Mill). In the Manitoba provincial public service, all levels of employees help to decide on and then to implement any new office technology. And in the federal government, the Innovative Management Practices Group of the Personnel Policy Branch of Treasury Board advocates "multidisciplinary teams to ensure that human and social factors are given as much weight as technical considerations in developing new systems" (Brunet, 1985).

Finally, a number of organizations have also used joint participative problem-solving committees to deal in depth with health and safety issues (e.g., Ford Glass in Niagara Falls, Kruger Incorporated in Trois-Rivières, and Whonnock Industries in Northern Vancouver Island). In early 1983, Whonnock Industries and the International Woodworkers of America established joint problem-solving committees in six of their logging operations, each with very different technologies. The committees were given real authority to make important decisions in relation to all aspects of their operations. In the first two years of the program, the number of days of injury time was reduced by over one-third and the costs of injury time were reduced by over one-half. By mid-1985, only four accidents had occurred across six camps.

Gains-Sharing Programs

An interesting variation on the parallel participative structure approach to workplace innovation is the gains-sharing or productivity-sharing program, such as the Scanlon plan or Improshare. These plans operate very much like participative structure programs, with the addition of a predetermined, carefully specified and monitored process for the group sharing of gains in productivity. They are different from profit sharing in two ways: payments are not based on profits but on productivity improvements; and profit sharing is most common in non-union settings (where it is often, at least in part, a substitute for a pension plan) whereas gains sharing has a particular appeal to unions.[1] In fact, the Scanlon plan was originally developed by a member of the steelworkers' union.

Scanlon plans were probably the first form of parallel participative structures implemented in Canada. For example, Hayes-Dana and the International Association of Machinists and Aerospace Workers introduced a Scanlon plan in their operation located in St. Thomas, Ontario, in 1969. As is standard with Scanlon plans, the Hayes-Dana plan has two levels of joint committees: departmental production committees and a steering committee consisting of senior managers from various departments of the company, the senior officer of the union local, and elected employee representatives. There are five production committees, one for each of the five zones in the plant. These committees solicit and process employee suggestions on any matter affecting the profitability of the plant. They also discuss such things as production problems, purchase of new machinery, profit margins on specific products, or any other issue related to the plant's profitability. They do not deal with matters covered by the collective agreement. The steering committee handles any suggestions that have not been resolved by the production committees, usually those that affect the company as a whole or involve major capital expenditures. At both committee levels, management reserves ultimate decision-making powers. In addition to the above committees, joint task forces are sometimes established to examine particularly difficult problems.

The Hayes-Dana Scanlon plan is also typical in terms of its reported results: marked improvements in productivity with concomitant increases in employee earnings, less turnover and absenteeism, a reduction in lost time due to accidents, better labour-management relations, better communications and relations between workers and foremen, and a generally less tense, more participative workplace (Nightingale, 1982; Mansell et al., 1978). In addition, job classifications were modified to make them somewhat broader to allow for more job rotation.

In addition, a major finding about these programs in general is that the "... co-operative spirit and the willingness of workers to accept technological change must be considered to be the chief advantages of the Scanlon plan" (Nightingale, 1982). It is not surprising, therefore, that there has been a renewed interest in gains-sharing plans in the 1980s (see Nightingale, 1982; Guillet, 1985). Indeed, as other forms of parallel participative structures meet with success, employees often begin to demand some form of financial reward for their efforts (Lawler and Mohrman, 1985).

Limitations of Parallel Structures

Despite the kind of success reported above, by the mid-1980s experience is beginning to show that there are some serious limitations to the parallel participative structures approach to workplace innovation. The following limitations have not only been reported in an extensive survey of American experience with quality circles (Lawler and Mohrman, 1985), they have also been observed repeatedly over the past five years by professionals active in the field across Canada – most certainly by the staff of the Ontario Quality of Working Life Centre.

Ironically, but not surprisingly, some of the same characteristics of parallel structures that make them attractive are ultimately their weakness. The first and most obvious problem inherent in parallel structures is the very fact that they are *parallel*. Since creating a parallel structure leaves the existing organization structure intact, it is relatively easy both to set up the additional structure and to dismantle it. Given this reality, it is quite possible for a parallel structure to be stopped regardless of what might be happening within the change program itself. For example, many a parallel structure has died as the result of personnel changes in management or political events within the union, both within and beyond the local level.

The second major limitation inherent in parallel structures is less obvious but more fundamental. One of the main reasons why parallel structures are so popular is that they are not only parallel but also relatively unthreatening to the existing structure of both management and union. Although, theoretically, participation groups could work to make basic changes to existing structures, in practice they usually cannot because of both their mandate and their structure. Most QC, EI, and problem-solving groups are not permitted to deal with issues related to corporate policy, basic management systems (e.g., the role of the engineering department), or the collective agreement. In addition, when most activity within parallel structures occurs at the "area" level, participation groups rarely have the resources to deal with, or often even to identify, many such issues even if they are not off limits. In practice, what this means is that once the groups have dealt with the obvious problems and inefficiencies in their area, they hit a wall. It is very common about two years into a parallel participative structures program for groups to complain that they are "stuck," that they have "plateaued out." Not surprisingly, getting stuck is an even more serious problem when there is a gains-sharing component built into the program (Nightingale, 1982).

When participation groups get stuck, there are three scenarios that are common. In the first scenario, as the groups slowly run out of substantive issues to discuss, the people in the groups begin to lose interest in the program. And as the output of the groups slowly drops, management also loses interest. Since meetings are costly to an organization, in such cases (sometimes after a half-hearted search for some new problem to tackle) all the parties usually "agree" to let the program quietly fade away. If the program has been heralded as a major move towards a new participative management style, its departure can often leave behind a lot of cynics.

The second scenario is more dramatic and more complex. A group that has been turned on by the participative problem-solving process and by its early success cannot always be easily turned off. Participation groups who have acquired a taste for change often want to deal with more basic, often more organization-wide problems and will become frustrated and angry if told they can go no further. For example, workers may want to start applying the democratic principles operative within the parallel structure to the day-to-day structure where they spend most of their working lives. Unions become anxious to deal with that particular management policy that has been causing them problems for years. And management often wants to start looking at the inefficiencies or costs built into such things as rigid job classification systems. When one or more of the parties become frustrated, they will usually begin to put serious pressure on the other(s), often in terms of "testing their commitment." If the pressure and/or frustration become too great, it is usually not difficult for either party to find some way to end the program. Union votes to withdraw from programs are quite common. Management usually has to be more subtle, but it is always easy to cut back on resources or even to anger the union sufficiently to force them to withdraw. If it is the workers who become frustrated with both union and management, they are most likely to give up and let the first scenario take over. However, if the program ultimately ends in the second scenario, it usually leaves a wake of bitter feelings (and unrealized opportunities) behind.

The third scenario is the most optimistic. Sometimes management, union, and the workers all agree that it is worth trying to bring down the wall. For various reasons (greater workplace democracy and increased organizational flexibility being the most common), they all want to shift the basic nature of the change program away from parallel structures into a redesign of existing structures. However, experience has shown this to be an extremely difficult task for three interrelated reasons: the wrong kind of prework has been done within the organization as a whole; the wrong structures have been developed (i.e., the wrong kinds of people in the wrong kinds of groups); and, finally, the wrong sorts of preparation and resources have been given to the groups. Given such hurdles, it is not surprising that only a few organizations have been able to move from QC or EI programs into more fundamental job and organization redesign.

The lesson from the above analysis is clear. Parallel participative structures can be an extremely powerful approach for dealing with many problems related to productivity, quality, technological change, health and safety, working conditions, etc. However, there are clear limits to how far such programs can go. In order to have a parallel structure that is "successful" in the long run, it should be defined and "sold" in an honest and realistic way. If more fundamental organization change is the ultimate goal, then a different approach should be used from the start.

Socio-Technical Systems –
The Effective Organization

The socio-technical systems (STS) approach is the most radical approach to workplace innovation. Its explicit ideal is to achieve the most effective and most democratic workplace possible. According to STS, organizational effectiveness and workplace democracy must be designed and continually redesigned into basic organization structures and processes. STS theory argues that the values, objectives, and methods of scientific management, upon which most current organizations are built, are not only autocratic but also inevitably lead to suboptimal organization performance. The following description of socio-technical systems theory is based on Emery (1959 and 1978), Emery and Trist (1960), Cherns (1976), and Trist et al. (1981).

The technical and human elements of an organization, in socio-technical terms, must be recognized as interdependent parts of the whole, which itself must be seen in relation to its external environment. The technical subsystem of an organization consists of the equipment, tools, and techniques (i.e., the ways the equipment and tools are organized, operated, and controlled) used to convert inputs into outputs. The social subsystem includes the division and co-ordination of work (e.g., jobs, roles, lines of authority) as well as decision-making and dispute resolution processes and mechanisms for maintaining the organization over time (e.g., recruitment, training). For an organization to be optimally effective (i.e., to come as close as possible to achieving its ideals), not only do both the technical and social subsystems each have to be effective in and of themselves, but, more importantly, they must be co-designed to fit together in such a way as to accommodate and support each other. According to STS, the demands of both subsystems must be met, but there is a choice as to how this can be done. The choice rests within *both* subsystems and within the connections between the two. Thus, the socio-technical systems approach is a non-deterministic approach, which argues that to achieve organization effectiveness, the basic structures of the organization must *directly* meet the needs of both the organization's technical system and its people.

The most fundamental need of the technical system is for variance control – that is, variances (basically, any unprogrammed event that can cause the input/output conversion to go awry), if they cannot be eliminated, must be controlled as quickly and as near to their point of origin as possible. The needs of people in relation to work, according to STS thinking, are for autonomy and discretion, opportunities for on-going learning, optimal variety, social support and recognition, the opportunity to make a meaningful contribution, and a desirable future. In addition, the organization as a whole needs to be able to constantly adapt to a wide range of unpredictable events in its environment.

In order to meet all of the above needs effectively, organizations must aim for maximum flexibility and integration vs. specialization and segregation; immediate, internal control of all variances vs. external control; and rule by principle (minimal critical specification) vs. rule by detailed regulation. In practice, what this means is that a high degree of self-regulation and participation must be built into the day-to-day operation of the organization. The same policies, structures, and processes lead *directly* to organizational effectiveness, workplace democracy, and a generally high quality of worklife for employees.

The basic building block of the socio-technical systems approach is the semi-autonomous work groups.

These groups are teams of workers who have collective responsibility for a natural, whole unit of work. The teams are self-regulating in that they exercise considerable autonomy in planning, integrating, executing, and monitoring the set of interdependent tasks within their work unit. As semi-autonomous groups mature, they also take on some of the support functions (e.g., maintenance, financial control, personnel, etc.) required for the functioning of their unit. Most workers in such groups do not have separate job assignments or classifications. Ideally, all workers in the group are multi-skilled and can perform all the tasks within the work unit. In cases where the complexity of the work allows for little multi-skilling (e.g., an R & D group), the group still controls its own internal and external integration.

The semi-autonomous work group is a powerful innovation because of the concepts of group responsibility and self-regulation. The group orientation allows for more variety, enhanced opportunities for learning, and social support – all in relation to an inherently meaningful, whole piece of work. However, the group orientation also greatly increases the flexibility and problem-solving capacities of the organization. Similarly, self-regulation means not only that the wide range of problems that always occur in a work system can be controlled more directly and quickly, but also that it provides for greater worker dignity and organizational democracy. In addition, successful semi-autonomous work groups mean that managers are freed to concentrate on crucial planning and integration functions that are often neglected in traditional organizations.

As a total systems approach, the socio-technical systems (or "socio-tech") approach demands that both the primary work system and all support systems be designed according to the same values and goals. Therefore, in a socio-tech design all of the "management systems" (such as finance, engineering, personnel, industrial relations, etc.) must be designed to support the characteristics of semi-autonomous work groups. For example, in order to support multi-skilling and shared job responsibility, pay systems are often designed to reward people not for the particular task they are performing, but for the composite of knowledge and skill which they possess. This approach to payment is often referred to as a pay-for-knowledge system. It is this focus on total system design that most distinguishes the socio-technical systems approach from job enrichment programs.

One of the most significant characteristics of the STS approach to organization design is the great emphasis put on the creation of structures and processes for on-going organizational, group, and individual learning. Organizations cannot adapt to an environment that is complex and constantly changing; groups cannot deal with new problems and develop new roles and relationships as the needs and resources of the organization change; and individuals cannot learn new skills and redefine themselves in relation to both the organization and the group, unless there exists a fundamental willingness and well-developed ability to change. One of the great strengths of the socio-technical systems approach is that the same organizational structures which require on-going learning for their survival (e.g., semi-autonomous groups and open, participative management systems) also have the characteristics (e.g., autonomy, open information, etc.) which stimulate and support on-going learning. In essence, the organization design is self-sustaining.

The socio-technical systems approach is becoming more popular in Canada as the need for greater organizational effectiveness grows more pressing. As discussed above, over the past five to ten years, many managers and trade unionists have learned that other less radical, more piecemeal innovations cannot go far enough with the kinds of changes required by current economic and social conditions. However, it is also true that the socio-technical systems approach is the most difficult form of workplace innovation to implement.

Both union and management have built elaborate superstructures around scientific management – not only at the level of the single enterprise, but also at the level of the social, cultural, and legal fabric of society overall (Woods, 1969; Jacoby, 1983; Katz, 1984; Reich, 1983; Hirschhorn, 1984). The socio-technical systems approach challenges not only basic union and management power structures, but also the very definition of what it means to manage or to represent workers. It requires a tremendous amount of commitment and moral courage to face such challenges. Finding solutions also requires a lot of hard, slow work (Mansell and Rankin, 1983).

It is not surprising, therefore, that the STS approach has been used most often in the design of new organizations in non-union settings (e.g., Proctor and Gamble, Union Carbide, CSP Foods, Syncrude, Shell, General Foods, MacMillan-Bloedel, CGE, Esso Resources). In new organizations many "old habits," at least at the establishment level, are eliminated. In non-union settings, however, the absence of a union not only does away with one set of sacred traditions, it also does away with the major source of pressure that would most likely be exerted on the sacred traditions of management. The fullest development of socio-technical systems theory might only be possible where union and management are both present and both willing to work jointly towards fundamental change. The most obvious limits of a non-union setting are in relation to optimizing workplace democracy (see Bernstein, 1976). However, it is also true that workers who have no independent power base and no neutral means of due process (central to job security) are probably significantly inhibited with respect to the risk taking and openness required for optimal social support and on-going learning. In addition, a strong union may be necessary in order for workers to develop and articulate coherent collective positions on important organization-wide issues (Rankin, 1986).

The STS approach has also been applied most extensively in capital intensive, highly integrated continuous process operations. Since variances can move very quickly through such operations and take on many different forms as they do so, response flexibility and speed are at a premium. Quick, high quality decision making and execution can save a lot of money and grief. This situation is exacerbated where the nature of the product itself requires a high degree of precision. It is, therefore, not surprising that the socio-technical approach is most common in industries with the most integrated and complex technologies. Such considerations were certainly part of the major reason why Shell Canada, Eldorado Resources, and Canadian General Electric all have used the approach to build new facilities.

The STS approach, however, is not limited, in either theory or practice, to any particular type of technical system or organization. It has also been applied in batch and warehousing operations (e.g., CGE, MacMillan-Bloedel, Dominion Stores, Willett Foods), in unionized settings (e.g., Shell, Eldorado Resources, Inco Metals, Xerox) and in numerous office settings, both union and non-union (e.g., Manulife, Shell, Westinghouse, Province of Ontario Ministry of Consumer and Commercial Relations, and several sites within the federal public service). There also has been considerable success in the United States, Sweden, and Italy in applying the STS theory in the auto industry.

Probably the best-known and best illustration of the socio-technical systems approach to workplace design in Canada is the Shell Chemical plant in Sarnia, Ontario. The design of this plant is so radical and so successful that people regularly come from around the world to visit it. The plant, which came on stream in early 1979, is a continuous process operation that produces polypropylene and iso-propyl alcohol. The plant employs approximately 210 people and cost $200 million to build. The plant is highly automated, its technical system is complex and highly integrated, and its production processes require extremely careful attention to ensure acceptable product quality and plant and community safety. The plant is organized by the Energy and Chemical Workers Union (ECWU Local 800). The original organization design and its on-going redesign have been very much a joint union-management effort. The following description of the design and operation of the plant is based on Halpern (1984 and 1985), Davis and Sullivan (1980), and Rankin (1986).

The entire plant functions as a single operating department which is run at all times by a 19-to-21-person process team. There are a total of six process teams who work 12-hour shifts and are supported by one craft team composed of 18 journeyman craftsmen who work days only, Monday to Friday. All teams function as semi-autonomous or self-regulating work groups. The process teams are multi-skilled, that is, all members of the team are trained to be able to operate any part of the production process. In addition, each operator also possesses a second skill in a support function (i.e., quality control, scheduling, warehousing, or maintenance). Teams are, therefore, able to handle routine maintenance and quality control themselves. Five years after the plant start-up, the average team member was able to perform 70 per cent of the tasks required to operate the plant. The craft team is responsible for non-routine maintenance and for training those operators whose second skill is a craft.

The classification and pay systems of the plant are designed to support the multi-skilling concept. There is no hierarchy of job classifications. Operators rotate jobs and are paid on the basis of demonstrated knowledge and skill, in both the process and second skill areas ("pay-for-knowledge"). The more they learn, the more they are paid. There is no limit to how many operators can reach the top payrate. As of early 1985, 70 per cent of the operators were at the top rate. The estimated average time from entry level to top rate is seven years. A modified pay system has also recently been developed for the craft team to take into account their additional training responsibilities.

Each team in the plant is responsible for its own work assignment, technical training, overtime scheduling and authorization, and vacation scheduling. The first-line supervisor has been replaced by a co-ordinator who acts as a resource person and facilitator to the team and represents the interests of management on the team. Teams interview and hire new members from a short list provided by management and also play a large role in the selection of co-ordinators.

The management systems of the chemical plant have also been designed to support integration, flexibility, and self-regulation. A level of management has been removed completely and the jurisdictional boundaries between process and maintenance have been eliminated. The total plant is managed by two operating managers who are jointly responsible for the overall well-being of the plant.

In addition, there are significant innovations in the technical system of the plant. Many changes were made to physical layout in order to support the above design characteristics and to eliminate artificial status barriers. For example, there is a single parking lot with no reserved spaces, a single lunchroom, and offices are sized and furnished according to need, not status. In addition, new automated processes were designed to eliminate some particularly dull jobs.

The most important innovation in the technical system is in the communications and information network. The computer system provides direct information at various levels in the organization in forms and frequencies that would never occur in traditional plants. The computer is programmed to help operators learn what combination of variables are most effective in controlling the technical process. The computer provides the process operator directly with all available information, including financial information, on the condition of the process and the effects of variables at different control levels. The operator is left to decide which of various alternative actions is most appropriate. Craft team members have similar access to information and autonomy in decision making. Traditionally, such high levels of operating discretion and access to technical and economic information are the exclusive territory of specialists in engineering and planning functions.

All of the plant's support systems are designed to strengthen its basic design. Appropriate changes have been made over traditional design in hours of work, recruitment and orientation procedures, training programs, etc. Perhaps the most remarkable changes have been made in the collective bargaining system. Both union and management agreed that a collective agreement composed of tight rules and regulations designed to cover all possibilities was inconsistent with a design aimed at flexibility, grass-roots decision making, and on-going learning. Therefore, a contract was negotiated that specified only the absolute minimum, hence, providing a framework and set of guidelines for the employees to work within. Many of the rules of behaviour (called norms) are negotiated on an on-going basis between local union and management.

Finally, a special form of "support system," which is inherent in the socio-technical systems concept, has been developed at the Shell Chemical plant. A very effective set of structures and processes exist in the plant to support its on-going redesign. According to socio-technical theory, there is no one right design that should be put in place and forever maintained. As conditions change, both within and beyond the organization, the organization must also change. In the Shell Chemical plant there are many joint groups, both permanent and temporary, that are responsible for monitoring all aspects of the plant to ensure that the needs of the total system are still being met. Change is accepted as a way of life. Since 1979, the union, management, and employees have worked together to redesign such features as work schedules, mechanisms for distributing overtime, progression pay systems, staffing complement, performance standards, quality control procedures, staffing in the warehouse, training procedures, and methods for selecting supervisors.

In 1983/84, Shell and the ECWU conducted an in-depth analysis to assess the costs/benefits of the plant's innovative design. The results were impressive:

> The advantages of having multi-skilled personnel proficient in plant operations and equipment repair are most evident. Significant savings are being realized:
>
> – Many overtime callouts are avoided. Shift team members are able to respond to emergencies that arise.
>
> – Shift team members can use second skills on shift to perform non-emergency work that otherwise would be left to be done on days.
>
> – Maintenance work performed during shutdowns by shift team members reduces the need for contract personnel.
>
> – Plan shutdowns are avoided because shift team members can quickly correct emergency situations.
>
> In addition, quality control, handled entirely by operating personnel, is excellent. Throughput and on-stream time are substantially above design – attributable in large part to operator versatility and competence and dedicated teamwork. The absenteeism in this plant is the lowest of any of Shell Canada's operating facilities. The polypropylene plant's capacity has recently been formally re-rated to satisfy catalyst royalty requirements, by 30%.
>
> There is widespread participation in all matters. Ad hoc task force output is extensive and of high quality.
>
> In the more than six years since plant start up, there have been only 11 formal grievances raised in the chemical plant, none in the past 2-1/2 years. This compares very well with more than 150 grievances, with several arbitration cases, in the neighboring, traditional plant over the same period.

Inspired by the outcome at Sarnia, Shell Canada has followed similar approaches at several other sites. Socio-technical systems designs have been implemented for a gas plant, an in-situ oil sand unit, a fiberglass-tank-manufacturing facility, a lube and grease plant, a coal mine, a word processing department, a research laboratory, and most recently, a new $1.4 billion oil refinery and styrene-monomer complex in Edmonton (Halpern, 1985).

In addition, there is ample evidence that the design has supported the development of an exceptionally active, competent, and strong local union (*QWL Focus*, 1984; Rankin, 1986).

Although the new plant, or "greenfield," situation probably provides the best setting for developing a fundamentally different organization design, there have also been several applications of the socio-technical systems concept within existing organizations in Canada. Although these redesigns have been much more limited in scope, they have, nonetheless, produced quite significant results.

Eldorado Resources, in Port Hope, and the United Steelworkers Locals 13173 and 8562 have been active in redefining their relationship and redesigning their organization since 1979. Their program began with an intergroup (relationships by objectives) process designed to deal with what had been a very poor labour relations history. The intergroup process was very successful in improving union-management relations, but the departmental level joint problem-solving groups established in 1981 as an offshoot soon ran out of issues and energy. At that point, union and management established a joint QWL program focusing on the democratization of the workplace. Their first project was to develop an innovative organization structure for a new uranium refinery being built as a part of the existing Port Hope facility. The new refinery, which started up in June 1984, was designed according to socio-technical systems principles and has many of the same features as the Shell Chemical plant – self-regulating shift teams, multi-skilling, a pay-for-knowledge system, a single job classification, continuous training, a change in the role of "supervisors," and a reduction in the levels of management. What is most impressive is that this design was implemented within the framework of an existing collective agreement and was staffed completely, by seniority, from within the adjacent plants. Both union and management were willing to make the changes necessary within both their structures to enable the innovation.

Based on their experience with the "new" plant design, the company and union decided they would like to try to diffuse the socio-technical systems approach to the rest of the Port Hope facility. The first area to volunteer for redesign – on an experimental basis only at first – was the Technical Services Department. Before the redesign, the department was composed of two separate groups working out of separate locations and providing different services. There was a sampling and testing group performing one set of quality functions and an analytical group performing another. There was growing friction between the groups and signs that the department overall was not well connected to the total process it was servicing. Some job rotation had been tried, but without success.

A task force composed of managers and technicians from both groups was established to analyse and redesign the department. The goals of the redesign were to provide faster, better quality results to production and to provide more challenging jobs for people. The task force proposed that the Technical Services Department should be decentralized and a self-regulating team should be set up to service each plant on the site. All the members of a team would be trained to perform all the quality functions necessary within their plant. Implementing this proposal would require major changes in both the social and technical systems of the department.

In the fall of 1982, a pilot project based on the proposed redesign was set up within one of the Port Hope plants. After an eight-month trial period the members in the group had all been trained in each other's tasks, resulting in much more flexibility in servicing the plant and a great improvement in people's understanding of the needs of production. The bottom line was faster turnaround on lab results and more interesting jobs. In addition, the group was able to develop a new shift schedule to provide improved coverage and better working hours. On the basis of the success of the pilot project, the whole of the Technical Services Department was subsequently redesigned. And the socio-technical systems approach has slowly continued to spread as redesigns have also been done in both the janitorial and security services departments. (The above account is based on personal communications with union and management.)

A final example of a socio-tech redesign comes from a public sector office setting. Between January and August of 1983, the 20 employees in the Revenue Office of the Ontario Ministry of Consumer and Commercial Relations redesigned their operation. Using a form of socio-technical systems analysis, they took an operation characterized by a production line of discrete, fairly dull, repetitive jobs and built an integrated system based on four small, self-regulating groups. Each group is responsible for all of the functions related to a whole unit of work, including work planning and scheduling, allocation of tasks within the group, leave schedules, overtime allocation, and selection and training of new employees. In addition to the innumerable modifications to the technical system required by this basic reorganization of work, the group made a major technical change by totally eliminating one step in the old "conversion process." The new design also eliminated the need for one level of supervision.

The most impressive result of the redesign is that it is saving taxpayers millions of dollars in previously forgone interest by getting Revenue Branch deposits to the bank in record time. As well, absenteeism has been reduced by one-half and a chronic backlog of paperwork has been eliminated. The $15,000-a-year overtime bill for the Revenue Office has also disappeared. Not only do the staff report liking their jobs much more, they are also becoming more skilled – a benefit to both them and their employer. Finally, the union, OPSEU Local 516, has also benefited directly as the employees in the area have become much more interested and active in the union as a direct result of the QWL process. At the start of the program, the office did not even have a union steward; within one year, two employees from the office were on the local union executive (*Intercom*, 1983; *The Toronto Star*, 1984; joint presentation by union and management of the Ontario Ministry of Consumer and Commercial Relations, December 1983).

Misleading Labels

The above cases provide a good illustration of the strength and flexibility of the socio-technical systems approach to workplace innovation. However, a warning needs to be given to the reader interested in studying the application of the concept across Canada in greater depth. All is not necessarily as it seems, or as it is presented. Due to the high profile success of such companies as Proctor and Gamble, General Foods, and Shell (who consider that the socio-tech approach gives them a significant competitive advantage and who have worked hard to keep their innovations a secret), the semi-autonomous work group idea has become quite popular. Unfortunately, it has also become badly bastardized.

The language of the socio-technical systems approach is now being used widely to describe workplace innovations that bear little, if any, resemblance to it. Many organizations who have no understanding of, or commitment to, socio-tech are now setting up "self-regulating teams" or designing or redesigning their operation according to the "team concept." The socio-technical system concept requires that both the primary work system *and* support systems be redesigned on the basis of an in-depth analysis of the needs of the social *and* technical systems. Such an analysis is difficult work and requires commitment to fundamental change. Many "team concept" designs or redesigns are not based on any real analysis, but instead on a rather crude copy of what has worked at some other site, such as Shell or General Foods. Many "self-regulating teams" are not designed to improve variance control or organizational flexibility. Nor do they pay much attention to workers' needs for greater autonomy, discretion, or variety. The teams are set up more on the basis of similarity of function or geographic proximity and more as a means for achieving a group identity than for anything else. Members of the team often do rotate jobs, but the teams are usually given only very limited additional responsibilities (e.g., deciding who does what job). At best, the teams will meet periodically to discuss problems in their area. The basic structures of the organization, in particular its management systems, are left untouched. In essence, the approach is a form of job enlargement and/or parallel participative structure, disguised by a socio-technical systems label.

Socio-Technical Systems and New Technologies

Many proponents of the socio-technical systems approach believe that the basic, inherent characteristics of many new technologies are such that their fullest potential can only be realized when they are applied in a way consistent with STS (Pava, 1982; Davis, 1983/84; Kolodny, 1984b; Hirschhorn, 1984; Piore, 1985; Buffa, 1985). On the surface, this view would seem to be in direct contradiction with the concept of organizational choice, itself a cornerstone of socio-technical systems theory.

According to the concept of organization choice, given any particular technology, there is choice as to how it will be implemented in terms of the broader technical system and in terms of overall organization design (Trist et al., 1963; van Beinum, 1981; Skinner, 1979; Walton, 1983 and 1984; Davis, 1983). In addition, there is usually a choice with respect to the technology available to meet any particular organizational need (Noble, 1979; Skinner, 1979). From this perspective, new technologies can be used to create/support more highly controlled, centralized, bureaucratic organizations in which workers are de-skilled (for example, Bell Telephone; see Kuyek, 1980), or more de-centralized, flexible organizations where workers become multi-skilled (for example, Canadian General Electric; see McGill Human Resource Associates, 1985).

There are two key points to consider with respect to this apparent contradiction. First, there are many different forms of new technology and it is quite possible that they vary considerably with respect to the kinds of organization designs with which they are most compatible. Indeed, this hypothesis is currently the focus of a great deal of research in North America. The second point, however, is more fundamental to an examination of the connection between the socio-technical systems approach and new technologies. This is the simple fact that saying that choice exists does not mean that all choices are equal – either in terms of the values underlying them or in terms of their outcomes.

The argument being made for a natural connection between the STS approach to organization design and many new technologies rests on the belief that current social and economic conditions are making demands on organizations that can be met *most effectively* by adopting specific technologies, within a socio-technical systems framework. First, the expectations of the workforce in the 1980s are for greater autonomy, participation, and challenge in the workplace (Davis, 1983/84; *QWL Focus*, 1984; Guillet, 1984). Second, it is a generally held belief that the workplace over the next decade or so will be characterized by considerable ongoing change (Hirschhorn, 1984; Wheelwright, 1985; Kochan, 1985). Therefore, the strong emphasis within the socio-technical systems approach on policies, structures, and practices to support on-going learning and continuous redesign are well matched to this reality.

Finally, many theorists and business people argue that current world conditions are forcing a major shift in the world economy away from market structures oriented to long runs of standardized products towards flexible production systems producing a smaller number of high quality, specialized products (Reich, 1983; Piore, 1985). Hence, larger economic pressures are forcing industry to adopt technologies and technical systems (such as computerized numerical control, flexible manufacturing systems, partly unmanned manufacturing, just-in-time inventory and production, etc.) that emphasize quality and flexibility. As David G. Vice (1984/85), president of Northern Telecom Canada, has stated, "We've found the most significant benefits [of computer-integrated manufacturing] are more likely to be found in higher product quality and greater manufacturing flexibility.... Economies of scale give way to economies of flexibility."

Hence, we return to the argument that the inherent characteristics of these new technologies make for a "natural fit" with socio-technical systems design. This argument has been best summarized by Davis (1983/84), a leading STS practitioner in North America:

> ... the fundamental problem inhibiting economic effectiveness is the glaring failure to adapt the structure of organizations and their jobs to the new ways of arranging work necessitated by the operational requirements of contemporary technology.
>
> ... Automated, high-technology systems generate work systems that are "stochastic" in character. While such systems provide desired outputs largely without human manipulation, they require human intervention when, unpredictably, steady state or stable conditions are upset. Work thus becomes *intervention* to adjust or correct, following diagnosis, in ... an environment in which the content and timing of necessary actions cannot be predicted (and planned) down to specifics, but only in general terms.
>
> ... Therefore, ... automated systems *increase*, rather than decrease, the dependence of the organization on its members for effective operation. Dependence increases because of the major consequences of discretionary judgements made by operators regarding whether and when to intervene, and what action to undertake. In such settings, managerial or supervisorial control of operators, rigid job descriptions, external motivation of subordinates, personal persuasion, individual reward schemes, and much that characterizes conventional bureaucratic-scientific management is simply ineffective. To effectively utilize high-technology systems, a new "high commitment" form of organizational structure is needed, one that recognizes and supports self-motivation and includes wide response repertoires so that *dependable self-regulation* is the norm rather than the exception. Such structures provide the response capability and the organizational adaptability to make high technology effective by maintaining a high continuous capacity that permits economical achievement of product or service goals.

The above argument for the connection between the socio-technical systems approach and new technologies is well supported by the case of Sweden. In Sweden a combination of market forces and the availability and widespread application of automated manufacturing technologies (such as computer numerical control, computer-aided manufacturing, partly unmanned manufacturing, robotics, and sophisticated material-handling equipment and methods) have supported the development of what are called "product focused" forms of work organization built around semi-autonomous work groups. Kolodny (1984*a*) puts the lesson for Canada simply:

> Swedes are nothing, if not pragmatic, and only with the extensive restructuring brought about by technological change could the questionable economics of work organization innovations be overcome. Now, as these innovations are increasingly a part of the production technology of the country, their

generalized acceptance and increased implementation seem assured.

There is also growing evidence that Canadian manufacturing is beginning to take this route in its bid for survival. Such diverse operations as Canadian General Electric in Bromont, Quebec; Westinghouse in Renfrew, Ontario; Kelloggs in London, Ontario; and Pratt and Whitney in Halifax, Nova Scotia, are all investing heavily in both new technologies and socio-technical systems designs. The management of these organizations believe that the sophisticated, highly computer-integrated manufacturing systems of their plants require a committed, multi-skilled, flexible, and self-regulating work force. As the senior vice-president of operations for Pratt and Whitney explained: "The reason is to develop the ideal manufacturing environment for the year 1990 or 2000. The aim of this combination of new technology and new style employee is nothing short of industrial survival" (*The Globe and Mail*, July 3, 1985, p. B6).

3 Fifteen Years Ahead: Prospects for the Future

As illustrated by the sampling of cases in Chapter 2, there has been a vast amount of evidence accumulated over the past 15 years in Canada to demonstrate that there is tremendous room for improvement within the workplace. From the more limited job design, and communications and consultation programs, to the comprehensive socio-technical systems approach, the proof exists that significant benefits, to both the organization and its employees, can be achieved – even without large investments in new technologies, new marketing programs, etc. A mother lode of effectiveness often lies buried beneath a poor organization design.

What needs to be explained, given this fact, is why such workplace innovations are not more common. Notwithstanding the current popularity of parallel participative structures, most organizations continue to operate in a traditional manner. It is far too facile to say that the evidence is not clear enough, or that it has not yet been communicated effectively. While it is true that there is counter-evidence of innovative programs which have failed, often at considerable costs, financial and otherwise, much has been learned from these failures. A lot is now known about the conditions necessary for successful workplace innovation. In addition, many "failures" have in fact been programs that have been discontinued despite how successful they have been in yielding significant positive results.

Learnings from the Past

A lot has been learned, and well documented, over the past two decades about how to initiate a successful change program in the workplace (see Mansell, 1980*a*; Mansell and Rankin, 1983; Cunningham and White, eds., 1984; Bernstein, 1976; Goodman and Dean, 1981; Walton, 1980). If all the parties in the organization really do want change, there now exists a body of knowledge to help them to avoid many of the failures of the past. We know, for example, that active participation by all the stakeholders (more broadly defined than just union and management) is the key to implementing change. The program must be designed so that it is responsive to the needs and concerns of all parties. People need to see that there is something in it for them, and they need to know that they will be given the time, space, and support to work through problems they may have with the change.

Change programs also have a much greater chance of succeeding in organizations where they are supported by strong stable leadership within management and union. And union and management cannot work together effectively unless they have established a mature relationship based on mutual respect for the rights and sensitivities of each other.

A key lesson that has been learned about workplace innovation is that it is unwise to try to copy others. While principles and approaches are transferable, each organization must design its own structures and processes to fit its own needs. The various parties in the organization must also go through the important learning process that comes from having to work together to identify problems and goals.

In addition, change has not survived long if it has been limited to only part of the organization. The problems of "encapsulation" have been well documented (Walton, 1975). The kinds of change that are most likely to produce the most significant results (i.e., parallel participative structures and socio-technical systems designs) eventually need to be implemented throughout the establishment if they are to last.

We also know that change cannot be implemented successfully without a significant allocation of resources – in particular, direct funds, time, and, above all, people. The right people have to be involved in, and in charge of, the change process. People in key areas of influence within the organization must participate actively in the change. And the process must be led by competent people who are respected throughout the organization.

Finally, one of the most important lessons that has been learned about the change process is that it is not only intellectually demanding, it is also a highly political and emotional process. Despite what is known about success and failure, people cannot always be told what they "ought" to do – they insist on making their own mistakes. However, they will only be able to learn from their mistakes if they are prepared for, and able to cope with, some pain. This is one of the main reasons why workplace innovations need to be supported by strong, committed leaders and directly guided by mature and competent people.

Two important lessons have also been learned about why "successful" change programs have sometimes not been sustained. First, within many organizations, innovation has been regarded as if it were a product, rather than an on-going process. People have not realized that there is no one best design which will always be most effective. As the external and internal environments of organizations change, then any design must be continually redesigned.

The second lesson regarding the "failure of success" is much more fundamental. It is also the major explanation why more organizations have not become involved in workplace innovation. This reason relates to the fact that, in essence, any successful innovative organization is a kind of parallel structure within a larger context – whether the context is the total enterprise, the trade union movement, and/or society at large. In the same way that parallel participative structures are limited by, and put pressure on, the organization of which they are a part, innovative organizations are also limited by and threaten their environment.

Much of the innovation in the workplace, most clearly the socio-technical systems approach, is based on a fundamentally different set of values than are most organizations in Canada. The traditional organization design does not persist and prevail, however, simply because it is the most effective – a large part of its ability to survive is a function of the fact that it is embedded in the very fabric of the larger society. This is understandable; there would be no stability in society if the micro and macro levels were not consistent and mutually reinforcing. What it does mean, however, is that change cannot ultimately survive at the micro level unless supported by changes at the macro level.

Tensions between Workplace Innovation and Larger Society

There are two major sources of tension between innovative forms of work and the underlying fabric of the workplace in Canada. Both areas relate to the fact that union and management policies, as well as our industrial relations system overall, are based on the fundamental assumption that management will maintain control over the workplace (re methods of production, assignment of tasks, workplace layout, etc.), and the union will act as a "counter-organization" to limit management's control in specific areas, primarily fair compensation, job security, and due process (Adams, 1981). This assumption is inconsistent with the principles of joint control and shared responsibility central to the more advanced forms of workplace innovation.

Management Prerogatives and Corporate Policy

The first major source of tension lies in the area of management prerogatives and corporate policy. At the establishment and enterprise levels, elaborate management systems have been developed to support the role of manager as decision-maker and decision-enforcer. Selection, training, evaluation and reward, and punishment policies and practices are built around this definition of what it means to be a manager. A workplace characterized by participative decision making and internal control would require a redefinition of management's prerogatives and, therefore, of what it means to manage. Ultimately, such a redefinition can work only if basic management policies change – at the corporate level (Hirschhorn et al., 1983; Schlesinger and Oshry, 1984; Klein, 1984). While many organizations today are comfortable with "redefining the role of the first-line supervisor," or even the middle manager, they are not prepared to make the fundamental changes to their management systems overall that are inherent in any such attempt. It is, therefore, fairly common in programs of workplace innovation for first-line and middle managers to get caught between the demands for shop-floor change and the realities of a larger corporate system that is not changing (Hirschhorn, 1984; Schlesinger and Oshry, 1984; Klein, 1984). Not surprisingly, first-line and/or middle management resistance is often cited as the main cause for the demise of a "successful" workplace innovation.

Collective Bargaining and Job Control

The second source of tension grows inevitably from the fact that in North America the major vehicle of "counter-control" available to unions in the workplace is collective bargaining, the results of which are enshrined in a collective agreement. In response to the combination of management rights (reflecting the rights of ownership) and scientific management, over the years unions have developed a tight system of job control as the means by which to achieve job and income security (Perlman, 1949; Katz, 1984; Warrian, 1980). Job control has been won by specifying rules within the collective agreement to regulate every possible aspect of the job – from the content of the job and access to it, through to its evaluation and compensation, to the conditions under which it is performed.

Such a system of job control is clearly in direct conflict with an orientation based on minimal critical specification and maximum flexibility. However, it is also in conflict with an approach that gives groups of workers more direct control over issues of importance to them. As discussed earlier, it does not take long before workers begin to want to make changes to aspects of their workplace that are directly tied to the union strategy of job control (e.g., hours of work, job descriptions, etc.). That is, they begin to get into areas covered by collective bargaining. Hence, it is ultimately not possible to keep workplace innovation separate from collective bargaining. In discussing the growing demand of workers for more interesting and responsible work, the Task Force on Labour Relations (Woods, 1969) argued that:

> ... Unions, like management, have failed in this new and more challenging area, and to some extent this failure is due to the fact that unions and the collective bargaining process were not designed to handle problems growing out of the nature of work itself. It is debatable whether the process could rise appropriately to the challenge. Indeed, under some circumstances unions, if not collective bargaining itself, might prove a hindrance.

Seventeen years later, it is clear that union opposition has been one of the main reasons why many organizations have engaged in only very limited forms of innovation, if any, and why many more substantial innovations have died despite significant positive results.

Conditions for Linking the Micro and Macro Levels

Thomas A. Kochan (1985), who acted as a special advisor to the Macdonald Commission on the economy, concluded that the long-run survival of current innovations in industrial relations and organization design depended "not in isolating them from collective bargaining and corporate strategic decision making, but in linking them to the decisions and strategies adopted at these higher levels in our industrial relations system." It can be argued that there are three key interdependant conditions necessary for developing such links: 1) a significant amount of experience with trying to integrate new work forms and collective bargaining at the micro (i.e., shop-floor, establishment, and enterprise) level; 2) changes in the legal framework of collective bargaining; and 3) broader changes at the societal level that would support innovation by both union and management.

Experience at the Micro Level

Management's Response

Serious attempts to integrate collective bargaining and new work forms at the micro level will occur only if *both* union and management are interested in making more fundamental changes in the workplace. Management's interest in change seems to be growing fast. Although there are many managers who dismiss new work forms either as inappropriate and undesirable ("managers know best how to run things, workers need close direction and control, and unions are unnecessary third parties"), or as nice but frivolous in hard economic times, the pressures on management to innovate are steadily mounting. Harsh economic realities are forcing organizations to become more effective. As noted earlier, the imperative for increased productivity, better quality, and greater flexibility are leading managers towards parallel participative structures and socio-technical systems, whether they like it or not.

For the reasons discussed earlier, managers are more comfortable with parallel structure approaches to innovation. However, they are finding that many of their needs (for example, for more flexible production systems) require fundamental changes to existing policies and structures. Many of the changes that management most desires (for example, flexible job descriptions and work rules) are those that are most inconsistent with our current system of collective bargaining (Kochan, 1985). Quite apart from any anti-union sentiment, this is one of the major reasons why management is going non-union with its new organizations whenever possible. In addition, the absence of a union also means that traditional management systems need respond primarily to economic pressures, both within the organization and within the external environment, and not to many of the socio-political pressures that exist within a jointly controlled change process.[1]

Even in existing unionized organizations, however, the advantages to management of socio-tech redesign are so great that there is considerable incentive for them to consider certain trade-offs in the area of management prerogatives. In fact, many organizations have begun to integrate the socio-technical systems approach into their corporate strategic planning, for both new and existing facilities (e.g., Shell, Xerox, Continental Can, CGE, GM, Kelloggs, etc.). Like Proctor and Gamble, many organizations consider these innovations to be so crucial to their competitive position that they treat their activities in the area as proprietary information.

Labour's Response

Despite the growing interest of management in more fundamental change, very few attempts have been made to integrate new work forms and collective bargaining at the micro level (Shell/ECWU, Sarnia; Willet Foods/RWDSU, Kitchener and Ottawa; and Eldorado/USWA,

Port Hope, being notable exceptions). A major reason for this situation is the often negative, sometimes hostile, view of many trade unions towards the more fundamental forms of workplace innovation. At best, most trade unions are skeptical, hesitant, or uninterested.

Anti-QWL Positions

The strongest negative union statements about the kinds of innovations discussed here come from non-unionists writing "from a labour perspective" (e.g., Wells, 1983); from trade unions, such as the United Electrical Workers, who are ideologically opposed to any form of joint union-management activity (e.g., Turk, 1981); and from convention resolutions. The first two sources of opposition are understandable and not likely ever to change. Some individuals and a few trade unions who are fundamentally opposed to capitalism see these innovations simply as management and government tricks to "fine tune" capitalism (Hunnius, 1976). Until recently, these views have had little airing within the trade union movement. They have had some public profile because they catch the attention of the media and because publications and "public statements" have always been important tactics of their proponents. However, most unionists have paid little attention to them, and the trade union leadership has always made sure that the inevitable convention resolutions against QWL, etc., were defeated.

In 1983 and 1984, however, conventions of both the British Columbia Federation of Labour and the Ontario Federation of Labour passed "anti-QWL" resolutions. In Ontario, the resolution was passed despite the fact that more and more trade union locals were participating in QWL activities. Although the convention resolutions have probably had little effect on the activities of union locals who generally support workplace innovation, they have affected locals who are inexperienced or unknowledgeable in the area. More importantly, they affect, and *reflect*, the position of several key trade union leaders in relation to innovations occurring within the workplace at the micro level.

The support of the majority of the convention delegates for "anti-QWL" resolutions can be partly explained by the larger socio-political context of the times. A study of trade union attitudes conducted in mid-1982 concluded:

> The context of industrial relations, at the time of the study, is one of grave concern to labour, management and government. Issues such as inflation, unemployment, competition from overseas, low productivity, de-industrialization, and the impacts of new technology, coupled with a deepening hostility and mistrust on the part of labour towards management and government, creates a situation in which new initiatives, such as Quality of Working Life, are regarded with some skepticism.
>
> ... The picture which emerges is of a labour movement angry and pessimistic with regard to industrial relations (union/management, union/government) (Action Learning Resources Group, 1983).

During the economic recession of the early 1980s, many managers and politicians implemented and supported policies and practices quite antagonistic to unionists and many workers. Many managers resorted to old-style confrontation tactics in their dealings with local unions, pushed for concessions at the bargaining table (or simply took them in unorganized workplaces), and cancelled a variety of innovative programs as cost-cutting measures.

In particular, the 1983 B.C. Federation of Labour Convention took place in the midst of the Bennett government program of massive cutbacks and anti-union actions. Indeed, the trade union-backed program of opposition to the government, Operation Solidarity, was the main focus of the convention. In Ontario, the Federation of Labour Convention occurred at a time when the provincial government had passed legislation greatly restricting the rights of public sector unions – the very unions that are strongly represented at such conventions. In fact, the convention's resolution was actually aimed directly at the government-funded Ontario Quality of Working Life Centre.

The "unfriendly" socio-economic and political context, however, is not the only reason for the negative views of many unionists towards workplace innovations. There are two major reasons why unionists are suspicious of innovation: they distrust the motives of management and government; and they fear that innovations such as quality circles and socio-technical systems will ultimately weaken the trade union movement. Both areas of concern are very high in emotional content. Given the right political context, researchers and trade unionists who are ideologically opposed to such innovations have been quick to take advantage of the emotionality of the situation. It is interesting to note that both the B.C. and Ontario resolutions were supported largely by documents represented as objective research, but which in the case of British Columbia was built largely on many factual inaccuracies (see Gruntman et al., 1983), and in the case of Ontario, on two case studies only (see Wells, 1983) – of which one case was chosen specifically because it was *pre-identified* as a negative example of QWL!

Many labour people believe that management and government are only interested in programs that will benefit them in terms of greater productivity, ease of introducing new technologies, labour peace, etc. (Mansell, 1980a; Curtin, 1982; Gruntman et al., 1983). Therefore, they believe that such programs must be either of no benefit to workers or actually harmful to them. As expressed in the preamble to the B.C. Federation of Labour resolution, "There is little indication that the problems identified by workers will be dealt with seriously through the programs we have discussed.... QWL provides employers with one method of permanently reducing the workforce, introducing automated technologies while still maintaining control of the workplace"; and in the preamble to the Ontario Federation of Labour resolution "... QWL programs are often effective at convincing workers that cutting absenteeism, increasing productivity and reducing grievances are more important than correcting costly health and safety hazards, raising wages or reducing working time...."

The assumption behind these beliefs, often stated explicitly, is that workers and their trade unions enter such programs with relatively less power than management and do not achieve any real increases in power within the programs. This imbalance of power, it is argued, will inevitably lead to the abuse and/or co-optation of the workers. Trade unionists' concerns about their ability to control events within a change process are often reflected in negative statements about the process per se (van Beinum, 1985).

Of more fundamental concern to many unionists is the suspicion that new work forms will ultimately weaken the trade union movement. The preamble to the Ontario Federation of Labour resolution concluded that: "... labour's participation in the QWL Centre serves to legitimize this government program which is designed ultimately to weaken trade unions as effective workers' organizations...." This view has several bases. First, the linking of workplace innovations with "union-free" management strategies has led many trade unionists to see these innovations as anti-union. In addition, the stress placed by many theorists, managers, government spokespersons, and even unionists on the co-operative "win-win" element of these programs has led many to conclude that the programs rest on the assumption that there is no conflict of interest between management and labour. Conflict of interest between management and labour is absolutely fundamental to the existence of an independent trade union movement. Although these concerns have been countered by the existence of many successful innovations in unionized settings, and by a more realistic appreciation of the nature of conflict within new work forms (e.g., see Mansell and Rankin, 1983; *QWL Focus*, 1984), they still weigh heavy on the shoulders of the labour movement.

The most serious and immediate basis for labour's concern about workplace innovations, however, is the fact that indeed they *do* interfere with collective bargaining – the more fundamental innovations are a threat to collective bargaining as commonly practiced by union and management today. Hence, the argument has come full circle – workplace innovations cannot advance unless they can be integrated with collective bargaining; they cannot be integrated with collective bargaining unless unions participate actively in the on-going development of the innovations; and many unions will not participate in the innovations because they ultimately conflict with collective bargaining. The question, then, is: are unions willing and able to participate in a process explicitly designed to make some fundamental changes in our current system of collective bargaining? What benefits are there in such change for unions, and what conditions are necessary for their participation?

Labour Support for New Directions

At least two major unions have responded positively to these questions: the United Steelworkers of America (USWA) and the Energy and Chemical Workers Union (ECWU). In speaking of QWL and Scanlon plans, the public relations director of District 6 of the USWA recently concluded:

> ... During the last decade, trade union attitudes have evolved, as have Quality of Working Life programs.
>
> Many trade unionists now recognize the genuine QWL efforts, even though QWL challenges the traditional way which trade unions do business....
>
> Both these systems of industrial democracy present a bold challenge to trade unionists – a challenge that we must face if we are to grow and, ultimately, to survive.
>
> We can use these systems of industrial democracy to build better and higher than we have ever built before.
>
> We have traditionally built by using the palpable and demonstrable building blocks that materially satisfy our members and assure their continued support. These are the extrinsic factors, such as a reasonable wage, recognition of seniority, pension plans, insurance and welfare benefits, safety and health, and other tangible items.

We must continue this most important task, but we can also add a new dimension, while consolidating these extrinsic gains.

We must respond to the intrinsic factors that many of our members are now demanding. Such factors as variety and challenge, continuous learning, autonomy and the opportunity to use one's own judgement, recognition and support, a desirable future, and a meaningful contribution to society....

Surely, that is the challenge facing us and, surely, we have the skill and stamina to meet it. If we do not, we are vacating this vitally important territory to exclusive management control, and we do so at our peril (Guillet, 1984).

Based on this conviction, the Canadian USWA has begun work on developing its own "trade union QWL agenda." This agenda is based on two key premises: that "... labour must take this initiative in order for working environments to be re-organized in accordance with the conditions and parametres it defines"; and that "collective bargaining is the most important process in establishing industrial democracy. Its potential for dealing with evolving aspects of labour relations has not yet been reached. Quality of Working Life initiatives can and must be dealt with through the collective agreement" (Guillet, 1985). To date, the steelworkers' union has not yet integrated its centrally developed QWL agenda with the practice of locals that are engaged in change programs. Rather, its practice has been to provide the agenda as a suggested guideline but to leave locals to handle their change programs more or less on their own.

The union that has gone the furthest in Canada with integrating QWL and collective bargaining is the Energy and Chemical Workers Union (see Rankin, 1986). Its position on new forms of work organization also reflects another major reason why other unions may be hesitant about change. The ECWU recognizes explicitly that the values and concepts underlying such approaches as sociotechnical systems cannot be applied to the workplace without affecting union operations as well. As expressed by Neil Reimer, former national director of the ECWU:

> ...You can't go to an employer and demand less supervision if you don't trust your own members to think for themselves in the union....
>
> A few years ago, we had a meeting with 27 stewards at Shell Sarnia and it was one of the most rewarding experiences of my union career. I wanted to know about the human dimension, about how these young people were affected by working in a participative environment. It made such a difference that it shocked me. Each of these 27 stewards could sit down with a problem, analyze it, and develop a solution.
>
> That's my view of what the union's about. When we ask the workers to stand up, we mean on their feet, not ours.
>
> We are not asking people to be dependent on the union – what's the difference with being dependent on the company? The union's job is to help them become whole persons in an industrial society (*QWL Focus*, 1984).

The ECWU, at all levels of the union, has made a serious commitment to quality of working life. In the union's National Orientation Program, which is given to all its new and existing members, QWL is identified as one of the five major national programs of the union. In support of this program, the union has developed a national policy on QWL and the policy has been endorsed by its 1982 National Convention. Most importantly, ECW national representatives and local executives are actively applying the policy across Canada, very often at the initiative of the union. Where the union does become involved in change programs, it insists that they be steered by jointy controlled union-management structures, at both the local, regional, and national levels. The union at *both* the micro and macro levels must be actively involved in the program. As an integral part of this approach, ECW representatives have been trained to provide support to locals involved in QWL and the union overall has developed considerable internal expertise in the area of workplace innovation.

The Legal Framework of Collective Bargaining

The position of the Energy and Chemical Workers Union has been severely criticized by unionists who claim that it is naive and self-destructive given the realities of our current industrial relations system (Gruntman et al., 1983). Many proponents of workplace innovation agree there is some truth in the claim and argue that basic changes are needed in the legal framework of collective bargaining in Canada in order for workplace innovations to thrive (Bain, 1978; Mansell, 1980a; Lemelin, 1981; Adams, 1981). There is also considerable evidence for this argument in the experience of Norway and Sweden where changes in legislation were found to be necessary, both to make unions more receptive to shop-floor innovations and as a form of societal declaration of principles or values, sanctioning certain positions and making others less legitimate (*Labour Gazette*, 1978; Gustavsen, 1977).

Trade unionists in Canada have been quite explicit about some of the conditions required for their participation in workplace innovation, changes they feel are needed in the legal and social framework of collective bargaining. As summarized succinctly by the former Chairman of the Ontario Labour Relations Board: "The trade union movement is also skeptical of any management initiated concern for industrial democracy when only one-third of the Canadian workforce is organized and unions are bitterly confronted by employers on a day-to-day basis" (Adams, 1981). Hence, the position of the steelworkers in Canada, which is frequently echoed by many other unions and umbrella labour organizations:

> People who are seriously interested in job satisfaction will have to first tell me that they are in favour of strong unions, that they want all obstacles to union organization removed from the laws and that they want governments to make sure that employers keep their hands off the right of workers to organize (Docquier, 1977b).

More specifically:

> ...If the government's concern about Quality of Working Life is to be understood as a sincere policy direction, the introduction of sectoral or regional certification procedures for workers who want union representation is a step toward proving government's commitment to QWL and industrial democracy. Anti-scabbing and first-contract legislation would strike a further blow for industrial democracy (Guillet, 1984).

Other changes that may be required in legislation before unions are able to participate more fully in innovation at the micro level have not been so clearly articulated by the labour movement. This may be because these changes are more fundamental and even trade unionists are not certain of just how far they would like to go. Simply put, most trade unions will continue to feel compelled to exert as much specific control as possible (via long legalistic collective agreements) as long as our legal system continues to grant residual powers to the employer. As stated by a former research director of the steelworkers' union:

> ... there are major institutional barriers in the way (i.e., of job re-design), and not just on the Union side. In the area of collective bargaining and contracts, there are three areas which are absolutely crucial: 1) job classification; 2) seniority; 3) grievance rights. There will have to be found new ways to provide for employee rights and job security equal to or greater than under the old system, if we are to go forward. On the management side, the traditional 'residual rights' form of management's rights clause cannot be reconciled with the form of work organization we are seeking (Warrian, 1980).

Understandably, unions will resist changes that push for more 'flexible' collective agreements, since even the complete removal of the usual management's rights clause means little when those rights continue to be enshrined in the legal framework of collective bargaining. In a similar way, management will resist changes that might push for *adding* legally binding restrictions on management's prerogatives to collective agreements. Indeed, management in Canada has long opposed the idea of using legislation as a way to enforce or even support workplace innovation.

In conclusion, two other potential areas of conflict exist between more fundamental workplace innovations and our current industrial relations system. First, craft trade unions are threatened by the kind of multi-skilling common under the socio-technical systems approach. And second, even legal trade union status could be threatened by widespread employee involvement in decision making (Adams, 1981).

Broader Societal Changes

Beyond legislative changes related to collective bargaining, other macro level changes may ultimately be needed to support fundamental change at the level of the enterprise. Although many different kinds of change would likely be required in the long run, only three will be noted here to illustrate the crucial connection between micro and macro level developments. On the management side, many changes in management systems at the level of the enterprise may be dependent upon basic changes in the economy which would direct the focus of top management away from financial indicators of corporate performance towards indicators of productivity, quality, and market share (Hirschhorn, 1984).

In an equally fundamental way, trade unionists and workers would be more open to micro level innovation aimed, at least partly, at greater organizational effectiveness if they felt their needs for employment and income security were protected within society. Hence, many trade unionists have argued for "greater economic and social democracy in our society" as a precondition for real improvement in the quality of working life (Docquier, 1982). In specific terms, this would mean:

> ... any agreement to participate in the debate about enhancements in productivity ... must also seek to establish new mechanisms for the distribution of the new wealth generated as a result of major

improvements in productivity. A number of such mechanisms appear to be available, from a significant shortening of the work week without a loss in standard of living, to fairly radical shifts in the structure of taxation in Canada, to improvements in the structure of social benefits, to earlier and more prosperous retirement (Surich, 1985).

Finally, union-management relations at the shop-floor or establishment level must ultimately be consonant with union-management-government relations at the societal level. This conclusion was a major finding of a recent study of the perceptions and attitudes of union leaders in Canada (Action Learning Resources Group, 1983). It is also consistent with the observation that those countries where significant moves have been made towards greater industrial democracy at the micro level are usually characterized by "a long history of co-operation between labour and management borne out of crisis or economic reality... and a commitment to national economic planning which percolates a philosophy of power sharing downwards" (Adams, 1981).

Current Developments at the Macro Level

It is clear from the above discussion that the future of workplace innovation in Canada at the micro level is inexorably tied to the future of union-management-government relations at the macro level. As little as three years ago, this future did not look bright. In early 1983, a group of academics, on the basis of a sampling of the attitudes and perceptions of trade union leaders, concluded that:

> A willingness to work as equal partners on both the shop floor and at planning and policy levels are evident – but the prior condition of recognition, legitimacy and equality needed to tap this willingness was not considered to exist or to be politically achievable in the current situation (Action Learning Resources Group, 1983).

Consistent with this view, many managers and politicians were arguing for, and implementing (for example, the Bennett government in British Columbia), "back-to-basics" belt-tightening policies that essentially excluded any role for trade unions. Such a scenario would certainly sound the death knell for any significant workplace innovation in Canada.

Despite this situation, however – and partly in response to it – by early 1984, business, labour, and government leaders had all begun to talk openly of the need for greater "dialogue" between the three parties. The severity of the economic situation and the above political reactions, as painfully experienced by all parties during the early 1980s, seem to have pushed them to take a serious look at new possibilities for dealing with the country's future. As rather baldly put by the Canadian Manufacturers' Association (1984):

> If the various sectors of Canadian society do not get together and develop a national consensus so that public and private institutions can formulate complementary plans of action, the chances of successfully competing in the global village are slim and our standard of living will fall.

Numerous speeches by business, government, and labour leaders over the past two years have reiterated the above view (see White, 1984; Armstrong, 1984; McKnight, 1985).

In response to these concerns, several forms of bipartite, tripartite, or multipartite "consultative mechanisms" have been established across Canada – at the federal, provincial, and sectoral levels.[2] At the federal level, the Canadian Labour Market and Productivity Centre (CLMPC) was established in 1984. It is a bipartite organization based on an equal partnership of labour and business, supported by direct input from senior representatives of the federal government, provincial governments, and the educational community. The mandate and goal of the CLMPC is to search for a consensus on appropriate ways to improve growth in productivity and employment and to improve the functioning of labour markets in Canada. A major part of the Centre's plan of action has been to establish and support bipartite subcommittees of various industries across the country.

In Ontario, by early 1983, the senior level tripartite Quality of Working Life Advisory Committee had begun to turn its attention away from shop-floor workplace innovations towards more macro level issues, such as the state of collective bargaining and the competitiveness and productivity of its industries. Reflecting this change in its focus, by mid-1984 the Committee had formally changed its name to the Ontario Labour Management Study Group, and adopted the following statement of its composition, function, and objectives:

> A group of Ontario labour and business leaders who, with the co-ordination of the Ontario Ministry of Labour, jointly identify areas for discussion and study, with the aim of developing or responding to recommendations that could address perceived private and public sector needs to the benefit of all parties (Ontario Labour Management Study Group, 1985).

Since the late 1970s, the Quebec government has commonly used multipartite mini-summits and commissions to examine specific subjects of provincial concern. For example, in the spring of 1984 a mini-summit was held on the subject of new technologies. In addition, in early 1984, the Quebec Ministry of Labour established a five-person multipartite commission, the Beaudry Commission, to attempt to find a consensus on a less complicated and conflictual labour relations system, looking at such issues as certification, negotiation, arbitration, etc., including worker participation.

Finally, in the fall of 1984, the government of Manitoba established a senior level labour-management committee to act as advisors to its Economic Committee of Cabinet. From this group, subcommittees have been struck to examine specific policy areas, such as the labour market and social security. The establishment of a jointly directed Workplace Innovation Centre to deal with productivity and innovative approaches to workplace issues, and focusing significantly on new technologies, is also being considered.

It is too early yet to know how the above macro level developments will affect the future of workplace innovation at the more micro level. At least three scenarios are possible. First, the senior level consultative mechanisms have the potential to deal *directly* with the link between workplace innovation and broader societal change. Given their mandates and objectives, both the CLMPC and the Beaudry Commission should be at least attempting to do just this. For example, the stated objectives of the CLMPC include: "... a planned, orderly and participative process of adjustment to new industrial structures and to changing methods and technologies; greater opportunity for individual self-realization through increased access to meaningful training, education and employment; ... and to contribute to the development of more and better jobs and an improved understanding of the concept of work." The consultative mechanisms in Ontario and Manitoba should also be well-suited to making direct links between the macro and micro levels, given the existence of umbrella tripartite activities at both levels in these provinces.

The experience in Ontario, however, does not bode well for this first scenario. Unfortunately, the Ontario Labour Management Study Group has not used its experience as a QWL advisory committee to attempt to link the micro and macro levels. Instead, it defines its current focus on societal level issues, including the "endeavour to persuade a larger segment of the labour movement and the business community to work towards improved relations," as "issues *transcending* QWL" or, even more explicitly, as "broad *non-QWL* objectives" (emphasis added, Armstrong, 1984). In fact, the Study Group, in particular its labour members, is quite removed from the activities of the Ontario Quality of Working Life Centre. The disassociation from micro level QWL may reflect the concern of the labour leaders with the 1984 Ontario Federation of Labour "anti-QWL" resolution discussed earlier; however, the evidence is more to the reverse – the passing of the resolution reflected especially the disassociation of the labour leaders from QWL.

Whereas consultation and "tripartism" were political hot potatoes in the mid-1970s when the Ontario Quality of Working Life Advisory Committee was first struck, by the early 1980s it was shop-floor level innovation that, for the many reasons discussed earlier, had become the politically risky issue. With rare exceptions (mainly the USWA, National Office and District 6, and the ECWU), labour leaders in Ontario have avoided taking any leadership position in the field of micro level workplace innovation. This has meant that the Ontario leaders presented no serious opposition to the Ontario Federation of Labour resolution and that much of the discussion on these innovations within the labour movement in Canada is being dominated by "anti-QWL" forces, who have made it a priority. In fact, the only information on the topic being offered to most trade unionists is being given by non-labour people, usually academics unfamiliar with the actual practice of QWL, who teach at labour schools. Even the many trade unionists with direct experience with innovation are generally not being asked to share their experience and knowledge. As long as this situation persists, it is unlikely that trade unionists in macro level bipartite or tripartite groups will be comfortable with the kinds of discussions necessary to begin to make *direct* links between the micro and macro levels.

In the second scenario, it is possible that senior level consultative groups could attempt to make changes which, while not dealing directly with lower level innovation, would be consistent with and supportive of it. In this respect, merely the existence of a societal level openness to more dialogue and cooperation is supportive of micro level workplace innovation. Given the kinds of issues being discussed at the macro level, such as the nature of collective bargaining, productivity improvement, and the introduction of new technologies, this scenario would seem quite probable.

A final, more pessimistic scenario should also be noted. It is possible that senior level government, labour, and business people could co-operate in an attempt to protect society against fundamental change.[3] For example, they might focus their attentions on trying to obtain economic policies (e.g., tariffs and import restrictions) that would buffer Canada somewhat against the pressures of world competition. The likelihood of this scenario is a function of the strength of the economic, social, and political forces supporting (perhaps forcing) change, combined with how much the current leadership is willing to pay to maintain the status quo.

Ultimately, the question of which scenario will prevail in Canada will probably be significantly affected by the opportunities and challenges presented by new technologies. Technological change is an issue of fundamental concern to business, government, and labour. It is also an issue that has widespread implications at both the micro level of the workplace and the macro level of society overall. The inevitability of large-scale change in relation to new technology, as well as possible inherent characteristics of certain technologies, may well "force" labour leaders to join business in exploring new forms of work organization – despite the difficulties they may face in doing so. In addition, the breadth and depth of many of the changes associated with new technology may make it virtually impossible for labour, business, and government leaders not to deal directly with the links between micro and macro level developments.

4 Concluding Remarks

The workplace in Canada will change dramatically over the next 15 years. That much seems inevitable. The economic, social, and political pressures being experienced in the mid-1980s must be addressed. However, the direction of the change is uncertain. Despite the success that has been demonstrated by many companies and unions with innovative work forms, their long-term survival and wider diffusion now depend on senior level leadership from management, labour, and government.

If the parties are prepared to work together to search for new answers to some very difficult problems, technological change may provide one key to achieving significant improvements in both the workplace and society, to the benefit of all. However, the benefits will not be without cost. The kinds of fundamental change involved in, and required by, the combination of new technologies and a new approach to the organization of work will not be easy for anyone. To advance further, vision and moral courage will be required.

Notes

CHAPTER 2

1 Profit sharing has attracted relatively little attention in Canada, despite the growing interest in profit sharing in the United States. A 1982 survey by the Toronto Stock Exchange of its 821 listed companies revealed only 15 companies with any form of profit-sharing plan – nine of which were deferred profit-sharing plans. The federal government estimates that 90 per cent of the deferred profit-sharing plans registered in 1981 had no more than three members and these were basically principal shareholders of the corporation. As of 1982, there were only 150 members of the Profit-Sharing Council of Canada with broad-based plans (i.e., including all, or most employees). Most profit-sharing companies, certainly the better-known ones, are non-unionized (e.g., Supreme Aluminum, Britex, Lincoln Electric, Dofasco, Canadian Tire). See Nightingale (1982) and Toronto Stock Exchange (1983).

Proponents of profit sharing argue that, as a form of economic participation, it improves employee motivation and enhances employee-employer co-operation. They also argue that the combination of profit sharing, employee ownership (normally in the form of employee stock ownership plans), and democratic decision-making structures makes for a "fully democratic" workplace. In Canada, however, most experience with this combination occurs in non-union companies where the democratic decision-making structures are employee-management committees, often called councils, that provide no independent base for employee influence. In Canada, when some form of "economic participation" has been considered (or demanded sometimes, by the employees or union) in conjunction with participation in decision making, the interest has almost always been in productivity sharing, not profit sharing. Profits are generally considered too much outside the control of employees. For further information on profit sharing and employee ownership, the reader is referred to Nightingale (1982).

CHAPTER 3

1 It is an interesting reflection on the field of workplace innovation that very little, if anything, has been written (or even discussed) about how the development of the socio-technical systems approach has been (or might be) hindered by the absence of a union. In contrast, much has been said about how the presence of a union can hinder its development. However, it can be argued that a strong independent union is necessary in order for both the technical and social dimensions of the organization to reflect the new set of values as fully as possible. For example, we might have seen much more work in fitting technology to people's needs if unions had been more active in the earliest stages of new plant designs.

2 A particularly interesting sectoral level development was the tripartite Canadian Steel Trade Conference held in May 1985. After two days of private talks, Canadian USWA and industry leaders established four joint committees to deal with offshore imports, technological change and labour adjustment, preservation of a fair trading relationship with the United States and continued access to its markets, and the status and future of the steel-consuming industries. This conference was the first time union and management had met outside the bargaining table to discuss their industry's future.

3 In this regard, it is interesting to note that the increase in societal level "dialogue" in Ontario has been paralleled by a noticeable decrease in the activity of the Ontario Quality of Working Life Centre.

Glossary

Computer-integrated manufacturing (CIM). Concept of the totally automated factory in which all manufacturing processes are integrated and controlled by central computer.

Computerized numerical control (CNC). Linking of several numerical control (NC) machines via a data transmission network under central computer control.

Flexible manufacturing system (FMS). Machines interconnected by transport system and controlled by central computer; allows variety of parts to be processed at same time.

Gains sharing. Schemes that allow workers to share the gains from increased productivity by earning a bonus; they include Improshare and the Rucker and Scanlon plans. Also called productivity sharing.

Job enlargement. Approach where a number of different tasks, all requiring basically the same level of skill and responsibility, are combined to enlarge the individual job.

Job enrichment. Approach where the skill level and authority of an individual job is increased through expanding the job to include responsibilities in such areas as planning, scheduling, administration, quality control, etc.

Job redesign. Number of related approaches, including job enlargement and job enrichment, that attempt to improve the intrinsic character of individual jobs.

Job rotation. System where a group of workers rotate amongst a set of distinct jobs, where the nature of the individual jobs themselves is not changed.

Just-in-time inventory management. Reduction of inventory levels through delivery of parts to assembly line as needed.

Parallel participative structures. Approach where an additional set of structures (usually some form of committee[s]) is set up, *in addition* to the existing organization structure, as a means of allowing for union and/or employee participation in a range of issues. The structures are "parallel" in the sense that the organization is not redesigned to eliminate (or significantly modify) those structures that would normally deal with the issues considered within the more participative structures. Includes program under many labels – e.g., QC circles, employee involvement (EI), joint problem-solving groups, QWL, participative management, etc.

Quality control (QC) circles. Small groups of workers who meet on a regular basis to help identify, and often resolve, productivity and quality problems related to their work area.

Quality of working life (QWL). Umbrella term used (most commonly in the 1970s) to cover many innovative approaches, focusing on everything from union-management co-operation, to job design, to worker participation, to quality circles. Common threads are a "shop-floor" focus and a concern for the qualitative aspects of the work experience.

Scientific management. Approach to the design of organizations and jobs that stresses the maximum simplification and specification of tasks, the specialization of functions, the separation of planning and execution, and the use of external co-ordination and control mechanisms. Also called Taylorism.

Semi-autonomous work groups (SAWG). Teams of workers who have collective responsibility for a natural, whole unit of work. They are self-regulating in that they exercise considerable autonomy in planning, integrating, executing, and monitoring the set of interdependent tasks within their work unit. Usually associated with the STS approach.

Social system. Includes the division and co-ordination of work (e.g., jobs, roles, lines of authority), decision making, and dispute resolution processes and mechanisms for maintaining the organization over time (e.g., recruitment and training).

Socio-technical systems (STS). Approach to the design of organizations and jobs that is based on the belief that optimal organizational effectiveness depends on a holistic approach that considers not only the needs of both the technical and social subsystems, but also the links between the two systems. Has both greater organizational effectiveness and greater organizational democracy as explicit values bases (see page 12).

Statistical process control (SPC). Use of basic statistical concepts to monitor how consistently products fit engineering specifications.

Technical system. The equipment, tools, and techniques (i.e., the way the equipment and tools are organized, operated, and controlled) used to convert organizational inputs into outputs.

Bibliography

ACTION LEARNING RESOURCES GROUP. 1983. *Perceptions: A Study of Labour Management and Labour Government Relations*. Downsview, Ont.: York University.

ADAMS, G. 1981. "Industrial democracy: A Canadian perspective." Paper presented to the Canadian Institute of Advanced Legal Studies, Cambridge, U.K., July 31.

ANDREW, T. K. 1982. *Quality of Working Life Project, Canada Post Corporation*. Ottawa: Canada Post Corporation.

ARMSTRONG, T. E. 1984. "Notes to the Advisory Council of the Conference Board of Canada." Montreal, February 16.

ARNOPOULOS, S. M. 1983. *Particichange: A Quality of Working Life Program in a Chemical Plant*. Montreal: The McGill Human Resource Associates.

AUSTROM, D., and S. GRAFFI. 1984. "Managing smarter in Niagara." School of Administrative Studies, Brock University, St. Catharines, Ont.

BAIN, G. S. 1978. *Union Growth and Public Policy in Canada*. Ottawa: Labour Canada.

BARBASH, J. 1977. "Humanizing work: A new ideology." *AFL-CIO American Federationist* (July):8-15.

BENNETT, R. F. 1980. "A management perspective on the quality of working life." In *Perspectives on the Quality of Working Life*. Toronto: Ontario Quality of Working Life Centre.

BERNSTEIN, P. 1976. "Necessary elements for effective worker participation in decision making." *Journal of Economic Issues* 10:490-522.

BLUESTONE, I. 1977a. "Creating a new world of work." *International Labour Review* 115:1-10.

_____. 1977b. "Implementing quality-of-worklife programs." *Management Review* 66:43-46.

BROWN, D. R. 1978. "A quality of working life model." In *Adapting to a Changing World*. Ottawa: Supply and Services Canada.

BRUNET, L. 1985. "New guide on managing the human side of technological change." *Quality of Working Life: The Canadian Scene* 8(1):7.

BUFFA, E. S. 1985. "Meeting the competitive challenge with manufacturing strategy." *National Productivity Review* 4(2):155-69.

CANADA CONSULTING GROUP INC. (THE). 1985. "Interim report to the Human Resource Task Force on the Automotive Industry." Ottawa, May 22.

CANADIAN MANUFACTURERS' ASSOCIATION. 1982. *The Future that Works*. Toronto: CMA.

CHERNS, A. B. 1976. "The principles of sociotechnical design." *Human Relations* 29(8):783-92.

CUNNINGHAM, J. B., and T. H. WHITE, eds. 1984. *Quality of Working Life: Contemporary Cases*. Ottawa: Supply and Services Canada.

CURTIN, I. 1982. "QWL smooths the way for tech change." *Steelabour*.

DAVIS, L. E., 1983/84. "Workers and technology: The necessary joint basis for organizational effectiveness." *National Productivity Review* (Winter):7-14.

_____. 1983. "Learnings from the design of new organizations." In H. Kolodny and H. van Beinum (eds.), *The Quality of Working Life and the 1980s*. New York: Praeger Publishers.

DAVIS, L. E., and C. S. SULLIVAN. 1980. "A Labour Management Contract and Quality of Working Life." *Occupational Behavior* 1(1):29-41.

DOCQUIER, G. E. 1982. "Speech by the National Director, United Steelworkers, to the Canadian Council on Working Life Conference." November 1.

_____. 1977a. "Address at McMaster University." Hamilton, November 22.

_____. 1977b. "Address to the Canadian Association of Administrators of Labour Legislation." Saskatoon, September 13.

EMERY, F. E. 1959. *Characteristics of Socio-Technical Systems*. Document No. 527. London: Tavistock Publications. Abridged in F. E. Emery, *The Emergence of a New Paradigm of Work*, Canberra: Centre for Continuing Education, 1978.

EMERY, F. E., and E. THORSRUD. 1976. *Democracy at Work*. Leiden: Martinus Nijhoff Social Sciences Division.

EMERY, F. E., and E. L. TRIST. 1960. "Socio-technical systems." In C. W. Churchman and M. Verhurst (eds.), *Management Science, Models and Techniques*. London: Pergamon.

EMPLOYMENT AND IMMIGRATION CANADA. 1986. *Report of the Automotive Industry Human Resources Task Force*, Ottawa: Supply and Services Canada.

EPHLIN, D. 1973. "The union's role in job enrichment programs." *IRRA Series*. 26th Annual Winter Meeting.

GOODMAN, P., and J. DEAN. 1981. "Why productivity efforts fail." Paper presented to the American Psychological Association Meeting, Los Angeles.

GRUNTMAN et al. 1983. "B.C. Federation of Labour: Special Quality of Work Life Committee Report."

GUILLET, S. R. 1985. "A union perspective on quality of working life and the Scanlon plan at Nielon Casting Ltd." Paper presented to the American Society for Training and Development Conference, Anaheim, California, May 20.

―――. 1984. "A trade union agenda on quality of working life." Paper presented to the Eurojobs Conference on Productivity and the Quality of Working Life in an Age of Advanced Technology, Paris, September 13.

GUSTAVSEN, B. 1977. "A legislative approach to job reform in Norway." *International Labour Review* 115(3): 263-76.

HALPERN, N. 1985. "Novel organization working at Shell Canada facility." *Oil and Gas Journal* (March):88-93.

―――. 1984. "Sociotechnical systems design: The Shell Sarnia experience." In J. B. Cunningham and T. H. White (eds.), *Quality of Working Life: Contemporary Cases*. Ottawa: Supply and Services Canada.

HEMSWORTH, L. 1979. "Participation through communication." In G. Sanderson (ed.), *Industrial Democracy Today*. Scarborough, Ont.: McGraw-Hill Ryerson.

HERZBERG, F.; B. MAUSNER; and B. SNYDERMAN. 1959. *The Motivation to Work*. New York: Wiley.

HIRSHHORN, L. 1984. *Beyond Mechanization*. Cambridge (Mass.): MIT Press.

HIRSHHORN, L. et al. 1983. "Supervision in transition." *QWL Focus* 3(2):3-6.

HUNNIUS, G. 1976. "Co-determination: A capitalist innovation." *Labour Gazette* (August).

―――, ed. 1971. *Participative Democracy for Canada*. Montreal: Black Rose Books.

Intercom. 1983. "What is quality of working life?" 7(3). Published by the Ontario Ministry of Consumer and Commercial Relations.

JACOBY, S. 1983. "Union-management cooperation in the United States: Lessons from the 1920's." *Industrial and Labor Relations Review*.

JENKINS, D. 1981. *QWL: Current Trends and Directions*. Toronto: Ontario Quality of Working Life Centre.

KATZ, H. 1984. "The U.S. automobile collective bargaining system in transition." *British Journal of Industrial Relations*, pp. 205-17.

KATZELL, R. A., and D. YANKELOVICH. 1975. *Work, Productivity and Job Satisfaction*. New York: Harcourt Bruce Jovanovich.

KLEIN, J. A. 1984. "Why supervisors resist employee involvement." *Harvard Business Review* (September-October):87-95.

KOCHAN, T. A. 1985. "The dynamics of worker participation under collective bargaining." *Quality of Working Life: The Canadian Scene* 8(1):9-10.

KOLODNY, H. 1984a. "Product organization structures improve the quality of working life." Paper presented to the SME World Congress on the Human Aspects of Automation, Montreal, September 16-19.

―――. 1984b. "Eurojobs conference: Productivity and QWL in an age of advanced technology." *Quality of Working Life: The Canadian Scene* 7(3):6-8.

KUYEK, J. N. 1980. *The Phone Book: Working at the Bell*, Kitchener, Ont.

LABOUR CANADA. Various years. *Teamwork in Industry*.

Labour Gazette Special Edition (The). 1978. "Adapting to a changing world." Ottawa: Supply and Services Canada.

LAWLER, E. E. III, and S. A. MOHRMAN. 1985. "Quality circles after the fad." *Harvard Business Review* (January-February):65-71.

LEMELIN, M. 1981. "Trade unions and work organization experiments." In R. Dorion (ed.), *Adapting to a Changing World*. Ottawa: Supply and Services Canada.

LIKERT, R. 1967. *The Human Organization*. New York: McGraw-Hill.

LIST, W. 1985. "When workers and managers act as a team." *Report on Business Magazine* (October).

MANSELL, J. 1980a. *Dealing with Some Obstacles to Innovation in the Workplace*. Toronto: Ontario Quality of Working Life Centre.

_____. 1980*b*. "Labour-management committees: The Canadian experience." In H. C. Jain (ed.), *Worker Participation, Success and Problems*. New York: Praeger Publishers.

_____. 1977. "A critique of industrial democracy at Supreme Aluminum." *Labour Gazette* (July):325-26.

Mansell, J., and T. Rankin. 1983. *Changing Organizations: The Quality of Working Life Process*. Toronto: Ontario Quality of Working Life Centre.

Mansell, J.; R. Wilkinson; and A. Musgrave. 1978. *An Inventory of Innovative Work Arrangements in Ontario*. Toronto: Ontario Ministry of Labour.

McGill Human Resource Associates Inc. 1985. *Canadian General Electric in Bromont: Participative Management in an Advanced Technology Plant*. Montreal: McGill Human Resource Associates.

McKnight, W. (The Honourable). 1985. "Remarks by the Minister of Labour Canada at the 71st Session of the International Labour Conference." Geneva, June 12.

Nightingale, D. V. 1984. "Continuous renewal: Lessons from a QWL project." In J. B. Cunningham and T. H. White (eds.), *Quality of Working Life: Contemporary Cases*. Ottawa: Supply and Services Canada.

_____. 1982. *Workplace Democracy*. Toronto: University of Toronto Press.

Noble, D. 1979. "Social choice in machine design: The case of automatically controlled machine tools." In Andrew Zimbalist (ed.), *Case Studies in the Labor Process*. New York: Monthly Review Press.

Ontario Labour Management Study Group. 1985. *The Search for Common Ground*. Toronto: Ontario Ministry of Labour.

Ontario Ministry of Labour. 1984. "Ontario initiatives with respect to preventative mediation and quality of working life." Presentation to the Macdonald Commission, June 22.

Ontario Quality of Working Life Advisory Committee. 1978. "Recommendation to the Ontario Minister of Labour," January.

Pava, C. 1982. *Microprocessor Technology and the Quality of Working Life*. Toronto: Ontario Quality of Working Life Centre.

Perlman, S. 1949. *A Theory of the Labour Movement*. New York: Augustus Kelley.

Piore, M. J. 1985. "Computer technologies, market structure and strategic union choices." In T. A. Kochan (ed.), *Challenges and Choices Facing American Labor*. Cambridge (Mass.): MIT Press.

QWL Focus. 1984. "A labour perspective on QWL." 4(1). Published by the Ontario Quality of Working Life Centre. See interviews with Judy McKibbon, Gary McBean, Stu Sullivan, and Neil Reimer.

Quality of Working Life: The Canadian Scene. 1984. "Joint consultation: Achievements in the textile industry." 7(3):1-2.

Rankin, T. 1986. "Unions and the emerging paradigm of organization: The case of ECWU Local 800." Ph.D. thesis, University of Pennsylvania.

Reich, R. 1983. *The Next American Frontier: A Provocative Program for Economic Renewal*. New York: Penguin Books.

Reimer, N. 1979. "Oil, Chemical and Atomic Workers International Union and the quality of working life: A union perspective." *Quality of Working Life: The Canadian Scene* (Winter):5-7.

Rosenbaum, L., and B. Dresner. 1979. "Is job boredom really necessary?" *Canadian Business* (June):66-71.

Sanderson, G., ed. 1979. *Industrial Democracy Today: A New Role for Labour*. Scarborough, Ont.: McGraw-Hill Ryerson.

Schlesinger, L. A., and B. Oshry. 1984. "Quality of work life and the manager: Muddle in the middle." *Organizational Dynamics* (Summer):5-19.

Scotton, L. 1984. "Having a say in how the job gets done." *The Toronto Star*. March 17.

Sheehy, B. 1985. "A near-run thing: An inside look at a public sector productivity program." *National Productivity Review* 4(2):139-45.

Skinner, W. 1979. "The impact of changing technology on the working environment." In C. Kerr and J. H. Rosow (eds.), *Work in America: The Decade Ahead*. New York: van Rostrand Reinhold.

Strauss, G. 1977. "Managerial practices." In J. R. Hackman and J. L. Suttle (eds.), *Improving Life at Work*. Goodyear Publications.

Surich, J. 1985. "The productivity debate: A union response." *Quality of Working Life: The Canadian Scene* 8(1):3-5.

Toronto Star (The). 1984. "Plant layoffs forged a sense of purpose." March 17.

Toronto Stock Exchange (The). 1983. *Employee Incentives and Productivity: The Concept and Current Practice*. Toronto: TSE.

TRIST, E. L.; G. W. HIGGINS; H. MURRAY; and A. B. POLLOCK. 1981. *The Evolution of Socio-Technical Systems*. Toronto: Ontario Quality of Working Life Centre.

_____. 1963. *Organizational Choice*. London: Tavistock Publications.

TURK, J. 1981. "Collaboration in a 'partnership' approach, dead end for workers." *United Electrical Workers Union* 45 (May).

UNITED AUTO WORKERS. 1979. "UAW statement regarding QWL." Collective Bargaining Conference, May.

U.S. DEPARTMENT OF HEALTH, EDUCATION AND WELFARE TASK FORCE. 1973. *Work in America*. Cambridge, Mass.: MIT Press.

UNITED STEELWORKERS OF AMERICA. Undated. "Policy paper: Technological change."

_____, District 6. 1978. "Policy statement on the quality of working life." February 1.

_____, Research Department. 1982. "Towards a trade union QWL agenda." January.

VAN BEINUM, H. 1985. "What's in a name." Draft paper prepared for the Ontario Quality of Working Life Centre, Toronto, May.

_____. 1981. "Organizational choice and microelectronics." *QWL Focus* 1(3):1-6.

VICE, D. G. 1984/85. "Productivity and competition: The heat's on." *Business Quarterly* 49(4):53-61.

VIVIAN, E. 1983. "CMA turns to 'people power'." *QWL Focus* 3(2):12-13.

WALTON, R. E. 1984. "From control to commitment: Transforming work force management in the United States." Paper prepared for the Harvard Business School's 75th Anniversary Colloquium on Technology and Productivity, Cambridge, Mass., March 27-29.

_____. 1983. "Social choice in the development of advanced information technology." In H. Kolodny and H. van Beinum (eds.), *The Quality of Working Life and the 1980s*. New York: Praeger Publishers.

_____. 1980. "Establishing and maintaining high commitment work systems." In J. Kimberly and R. Miles (eds.), *The Organizational Life Cycle*. New York: Jossey-Bass.

_____. 1975. "The diffusion of new work structures: Explaining why success didn't take." *Organizational Dynamics*. pp. 3-22.

WARRIAN, P. 1980. "A union view of quality of working life issues in resource-based industries." Paper presented at McGill University, Montreal, January 28.

WATTS, G. 1982. "Management incentives: Trick or treat?" *Workplace Democracy* 9(4).

WELLS, D. M. 1983. *Unionists and "Quality of Working Life" Programs*. Rexdale (Ont.): Humber College.

WEST, A. 1985. "Pratt seeks new-style workers." *The Globe and Mail*, July 3.

WHEELWRIGHT, S. C. 1985. "Restoring the competitive edge in U.S. manufacturing." *California Management Review* 27(3):26-42.

WHITE, R. 1984. "Speech to the University of Toronto." Toronto, March 13.

WHITE, T. H. 1979. *Human Resource Management: Changing Times in Alberta*. Edmonton: Alberta Department of Labour.

Windsor Star. 1983. "Challenge of workplace: Helping people like jobs." May 6.

WINPISINGER, W. W. 1973. "Job enrichment: A union view." *Monthly Labour Review* (April):54-56.

WOODS, H. D. 1969. *Canadian Industrial Relations: A Report of the Task Force on Labour Relations*. Ottawa: Queen's Printer.